MY ENNEAGRAM

A Visual Guide to
Find Your Personality Type, Stress Less,
and **Live Your Dreams**

Abbey Howe

SASQUATCH BOOKS
SEATTLE

Printed in China

SASQUATCH BOOKS with colophon is a registered trademark of Blue Star Press, LLC

30 29 28 27 26   9 8 7 6 5 4 3 2 1

The authorized representative in the EU for product safety and compliance is Authorised Rep Compliance Ltd., Ground Floor, 71 Lower Baggot Street, Dublin D02 P593, Ireland. www.arccompliance.com

Illustrator: Jordan Kay
Editor: Jill Saginario
Production editor: Peggy Gannon
Interior designer: Tony Ong

Author photo by Ashlyn Kudransky

ISBN: 978-1-63217-568-7

Sasquatch Books
1325 Fourth Avenue, Suite 1025
Seattle, WA 98101

SasquatchBooks.com

CONTENTS

MY ENNEAGRAM JOURNEY vii
HOW TO USE THIS BOOK x
WHAT IS THE ENNEAGRAM? xiv

ONE: TAKE THESE QUIZZES AND DISCOVER YOUR ENNEAGRAM TYPE 1

ONE & A HALF: DELVE DEEP INTO THE TYPES 28

TWO: STOP THE STRESS & BURNOUT CYCLE 106

THREE: GROW INTO YOUR BEST SELF 136

FOUR: LOVE OTHERS BETTER 168

A NOTE FROM ME TO YOU 202
ACKNOWLEDGMENTS 203
FURTHER READING 205

My Enneagram Journey

It's the biggest audition of my acting career—a new HBO television series. As I stand in front of five total strangers, I can't help but feel that my entire life has led to this moment. No pressure, right?

But it's not *just* the desire to land this cool job that's weighing on me. It's also that, up to now, I have absolutely *nothing* to prove to the people who matter most (my parents—that all those years of driving me to voice lessons, seeing every single show (including that awful high school production of *King Lear* . . . sorry guys), and funding my theater school tuition was worth it. That *I* was worth it.

After doing a couple of scenes, I launch into the most nerve-wracking part of the audition: an a cappella rendition of Billy Idol's "White Wedding." But as I reach the chorus, something in me cracks. All the years of pressure—to be the best, to prove it was all worth it—suddenly feel impossibly heavy. My throat tightens. My voice catches. And before I can stop it . . .

I burst into tears.

I'm sure the casting people were baffled. Heck, I was confused too. For so long, my identity had been wrapped up in my ability to perform. If I couldn't succeed at this, then who was I?

I had never felt like more of a failure than I did as I drove home from the audition, ready to wallow in a bottomless pit of depression in my crappy Los Angeles apartment.

But then, something happened that changed the course of my life: I won an Instagram giveaway. (Yeah, I know. It's not your typical *deus ex machina*.)

They sent me a copy of *The Road Back to You* by Ian Morgan Cron and Suzanne Stabile. It was a book about the Enneagram, some kind of personality test. As a millennial from the BuzzFeed generation, I was immediately on board. I couldn't wait to read about a fun new way to describe myself—*Am I a Joey or a Chandler?* (I'm a Monica.); *Am I more like Belle or Rapunzel?* (Definitely Belle.)

But I was *not* prepared for what the Enneagram had to teach me. As I read through the book, I freaked out.

"How in the world did someone reach inside my brain and yank out my scariest, most vulnerable thoughts?"

Even more shockingly, there were other people out there just like me!

This personality typing system was like nothing I had ever experienced. Instead of looking at external behaviors, it examined internal motivations:

- *Why* do you do the things that you do?

So I asked myself:

- *Why* did I let that audition experience crush me so thoroughly?
- *Why* am I so afraid of disappointing my parents?
- *Why* am I even trying to be an actor?

The only answer I could come up with was "I don't want to be a failure." That's it. There wasn't passion or desire. Maybe there had been once. But now there was only fear.

Then I read about my Enneagram type's core motivations. (For the record, I am a Type Three. More on that type on page 47.) That's when a lightbulb went on in my head.

I had spent my entire life trying to prove my worth by impressing other people.

I couldn't voice it before, but now I saw clearly what needed to change: I didn't want to live in a world where my happiness and identity hinged on how "successful" I looked to others when I couldn't even define success for myself.

I felt like a new chapter had opened up for me. So I devoured that Enneagram book. Then another. And another.

At the time, I had a YouTube channel where I made sketch comedy videos about things I thought were interesting. Naturally, as I became obsessed with the Enneagram, I started making content about it on my channel—acting out the different personality types and how they might respond to different scenarios.

Comments started to flood in:

- “I feel attacked.”
- “I’ve never felt more seen in my life.”
- “This is me!!”

And my favorite comment of all time:

- “Did you become a bug and hide out in my room? How do you know so much about me?”

From the reaction my videos were getting online, I could tell that it wasn’t just me who was impacted by this personality tool. So I decided to get serious and get my certification for Enneagram coaching.

And for the first time, I found my own version of success: a life where I got to help other people understand their personalities while flexing my creative muscles through writing, acting, and shooting my own work.

Since then I’ve taught millions of people about the Enneagram—from the college student struggling to find a friend group (because they prefer to observe rather than participate) to the corporate exec who doesn’t know how to reconcile their blunt leadership style with the softer leadership needs of their team.

If you give it a chance, finding your type has the power to break you out of negative patterns and help you grow into your best self. I’ve created this workbook in the hope that you will have the same “aha” moment and transformation I had when I first held an Enneagram book in my hands.

This is the book I wish I’d had when I was crying in my car outside the audition studio, feeling like my life was over because I didn’t get a role. It’s the book I want to give to my nieces and nephews when they come to me for help. It’s an extension of me, your Enneagram BFF, holding your hand and leading you on a compassionate journey of self-discovery.

Happy discovering, friends. I’m so excited for you!

How to Use This Book

This book presents a four-step approach to transforming you into your best self, with actionable tips and exercises to guide your way.

STEP ONE helps you find your Enneagram type with two different quizzes. If you relate to multiple types, don't worry—that's totally normal! You will share traits with other Enneagram types, but you can only have one main type.*

STEP ONE AND A HALF After you take the tests, you'll immediately want to do a deep dive into all nine types so you can unearth your core motivations and discover your main type. This section is like a little informational intermission before you discover what to do with your newfound Enneagram wisdom.

STEP TWO dives into the biggest roadblocks to your growth—stress and burnout—and shows you how to tackle them using your knowledge of your Enneagram type. You'll learn to spot the warning signs before they take over and walk away with a personalized toolkit of coping strategies and growth tips.

*This is best explained by an experience I had on a scorching day in Bryan, Texas. As I was leading an Enneagram workshop, a woman gasped, "OMG, my husband is definitely a Five!" When I asked why, she said, "He got obsessed with making the perfect steak—his YouTube history was full of Gordon Ramsay videos. Fives love mastering their interests!"

Then a Type One chimed in, "I've done that, but only until I learned the *right* way to cook steak. Then I stopped."

I geeked out—this was the Enneagram in action! We might all watch steak videos, but our *why* is different based on our type. For example, a Type Two might want to show her family just how much she loves them by serving a delicious meal, but a Type Four might be motivated by the desire to create something special.

STEP THREE is all about leveling up! You'll get tips, tools, and exercises to help you grow into your best self, chase your dreams, and crush your goals. We'll dive into your type's core struggles and how they might be holding you back—plus, you'll learn practical ways to overcome them. You'll also explore your Enneagram wings and how they shape your personality, giving you a deeper understanding of what makes you *you!*

STEP FOUR is all about the people we love: how to better understand them, support them, and create stronger, more meaningful relationships. Whether you focus on family, friends, or a romantic partner, you'll learn how to apply your Enneagram knowledge to deepen your connections. If you've ever wanted to love and support the other types in your life in a way that truly speaks to them, this step is for you!

How to Move Through This Guide

When you begin this book, you'll find two quizzes that provide number results, which you should simply see as starting points. After that, every exercise, explanation, and insight is designed to help you uncover your true type with confidence. This isn't just another fast-food Enneagram assessment (you know, a quick and easy-to-consume online test that just assigns you a number and calls it a day). I've spent thousands of hours helping people uncover their true types, and I've developed my own method to make the process clearer, more reliable, and honestly, way more fun! No test can fully define who you are because you are more than just a set of answers. That's why this workbook looks at the bigger picture, guiding you step by step to narrow down your type while avoiding the common mistakes that make Enneagram typing tricky.

BE SURE TO MAKE IT YOUR OWN: When I was in school, I hated dense, dry textbooks. But give me a creative project to sink my teeth into? *I'm all in.* I'm talking about making a magnificent hedgehog sculpture out of toothpicks in 5th grade (still proud of that, tbh). So that is my hope for the book you hold in your hands: This is now *your* fun, creative project. Get out your stickers, Gelly Roll pens, and your favorite cozy beverage. Dog-ear the crap out of it. (If you're a book purist, please forgive my blasphemy; feel free to use a bookmark.) This is not a place for dust bunnies to collect. And remember—this isn't a one-and-done kind of thing. Come back to it when you're feeling stuck, burned out, or wondering if your new crush might be a Type Five.

RULES FOR THIS BOOK

Practice Compassion

This isn't a weapon to use against others to say, "Look! The guide clearly says you're messed up. Be better!" Instead, use it privately to better understand why people do what they do. Once you understand the *why*, behaviors make more sense, and you'll find it easier to access grace and compassion.

Take What Works, Leave What Doesn't

As much of an Enneagram nerd as I am, I've gotta be honest: No typology system can fully capture the complexities of your soul or brain. It was created by flawed people (aren't we all?), so it's not flawless. In fact, only the Big Five—which measures openness, conscientiousness, extraversion, agreeableness, and neuroticism—is considered scientifically rigorous, because personality typing isn't hard science. That's why I beg you not to treat the Enneagram as an authoritative doctrine on who you are as a human being. Instead, see it as a tool for self-understanding. If it helps, use it. If it doesn't—be like NSYNC and say, "Bye bye bye." To help with this, you'll find occasional "Take What Works, Leave What Doesn't" pages to jot down what resonates . . . and what doesn't.

Break Outta That Box

The Enneagram isn't in the business of sticking people into boxes. Like it or not, you're already *in* a box. Call it your comfort zone, your patterns of behavior, your survival tactics . . . you've been making decisions from that place for a long time. As you move through this guide, I challenge you to ask yourself: "Why am I doing this in the first place? And how can I break out of the box that I'm already in?"

What Is the Enneagram?

The Nine Ways of Seeing

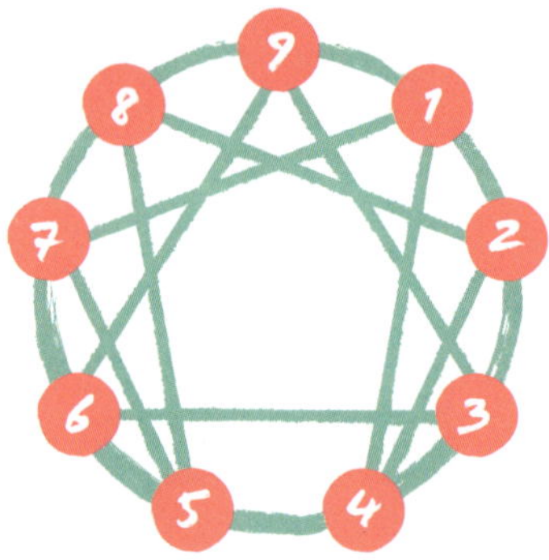

In its simplest form, the Enneagram is about the way you see the world. It theorizes that you view life through one of nine perspectives and that perspective shapes the things you do. These nine ways of seeing are the Enneagram personality types, which you can visualize through this symbol. The name "Enneagram" comes from the Greek words "innéa" meaning "nine" and "gramma" meaning "figure" or "drawing."

But I want to note: The numbers themselves are arbitrary. No type is better than another because it has a higher or lower number. They could've been letters, colors, or cute woodland creatures. (Now I'm really wishing that it was cute woodland creatures so I could be a Type Hedgehog!)

The point is that the symbol gives us a visual for this personality typing system while also telling us how the types relate to each other.

WHERE DID IT COME FROM?

I like to say the Enneagram is like my Great Aunt Hazel. We know she's old; we're just not quite sure *how* old. (I'm pretty sure her 29th birthday is the last time she ever revealed her age.) It's the same with the Enneagram. Nobody knows the exact date it first appeared, but we know a version of it has been around for decades, with some claiming that it can be traced back as far as the fourth century. Which, coincidentally, is when Great Aunt Hazel graduated from college.

The Enneagram as we know it didn't emerge until the 1950s, when a Bolivian philosopher named Oscar Ichazo shaped those earlier teachings into the typing system we know today. Then his student, Claudio Naranjo, an American-trained psychiatrist, brought the Enneagram to the United States and blended it with modern psychology.

But the Enneagram differs from other personality typing systems in that it can't point to a single creator or point of origin. Like, Myers–Briggs fans can point to the founders, Katharine Briggs and her daughter, Isabel Myers. Do a quick Google search, and you can discover how the DiSC Assessment was first developed or who created StrengthsFinder.

The Enneagram, on the other hand, has always been a communal tool. I think this is what makes it so beautiful: Each teacher approaches the system according to their personal lens. They may introduce new elements, discard others, or redefine existing concepts within the Enneagram framework.

So, like clay, the Enneagram evolves and adapts in the hands of its teachers. And this reflects the diversity of interpretations that enrich our understanding of ourselves and others.

In today's world, this tool is used by therapists, spiritual leaders, and more recently, large corporations that use it to improve conflict resolution, leadership tactics, and morale.

But perhaps the most valuable thing about it is how it can spark better, more thoughtful conversation by making you aware, possibly for the first time, of the unique glasses through which you're seeing the world. And even more importantly, you start to understand the lens through which your best friend is seeing the world! And your mom! And your boss! And your arch nemesis!

That's ultimately the goal of the Enneagram: It's a tool for transformation, for understanding yourself, and for better understanding others.

9
1
2
3
4
5
6
7
8

Type One

The Reformer

Ones are ethical and responsible people who spend each day striving to improve themselves and the world around them.

Type Two

The Helper

Twos are warm and generous people who build their lives around relationships and community.

Type Three

The Striver

Threes are driven, adaptable individuals who work hard to succeed and shape a life they can be proud of.

Type Four

The Individualist

Fours approach life creatively, valuing their ability to connect on deeper levels and see the beauty in the world.

Type Five

The Seeker

Fives are lifelong learners who focus their energy on gaining knowledge and competency.

Type Six

The Loyalist

Sixes are grounded, strategic thinkers who excel at troubleshooting problems and keeping themselves and others safe.

Type Seven

The Enthusiast

Sevens are natural adventurers, drawn to possibility, innovation, and anything that brings a spark of joy to their lives and the lives of others.

Type Eight

The Protector

Eights are powerful, no-nonsense individuals who fight for justice, stand their ground, and protect the people and ideas they believe in.

Type Nine

The Peacemaker

Nines are peace-loving souls who bring calm to chaos and have a natural ability to build bridges between disparate groups of people.

ONE
TAKE
QUIZZES
YOUR

THESE
& DISCOVER
ENNEAGRAM
TYPE

“When I discover who I am, I’ll be free.”

—RALPH ELLISON

1. TAKE A QUIZ

I've created two quizzes to help you find your type. Quiz One (page 9) will help you find the category your type belongs in based on how you navigate stress, emotions, and decision-making. Quiz Two (page 15) will help you uncover your possible types based on your core motivations.

But, and I want to emphasize this, please use the tests in tandem with the other steps we're about to talk about. This will make sure you end up with an accurate typing so that the work you do here actually makes a difference in your life.

2. ELIMINATE ONES YOU'RE SURE AREN'T YOU

Write down your results from the two quizzes, and fill out the questions on page 24. The goal is to eliminate some types that definitely aren't you and identify a few types that might fit. Then, read the descriptions of your finalists in the types section starting on page 28.

3. ASK YOURSELF: DOES THIS MAKE ME CRINGE?

Did you read about a certain type and cringe a little? I hate to break it to you, but the type that seems clearly like the worst type . . . is probably your type. (Spoiler alert: The "worst type" doesn't exist.)

4. UNDERSTAND YOUR WHY

I probably sound like a broken record at this point, but at the end of the day, it all comes back to the *why*. Which Enneagram type mirrors your internal motivations?

Enneagram Triads:

A Hack for Finding Your Main Type

We can group the nine types in many ways, but one of the most common is through the Centers of Intelligence triad. Essentially, this is a grouping of three types that have core traits in common. This is a *great* way to find your type because if you find your triad, you know your main type is one of those three. I like those odds!

The Centers of Intelligence triad is a way to categorize how you handle stress and feelings, and make decisions. You can either be a Feeler, a Thinker, or an Instinctive.

FEELERS

The Feelers are driven by emotion, reacting primarily from the heart. That doesn't mean they can't think logically or trust their instincts. It just means their first impulse is to check in with how they feel. These are Types Two, Three, and Four.

But here's where you can get tripped up.

Twos, Threes, and Fours deal with emotions *very* differently. So how can they all be triad roommates, splitting a pizza and complaining about how loud their upstairs neighbor is?

Just because your emotional impulse comes from the same place doesn't mean the outward behavior looks the same. For example, Type Twos get laser-focused on the feelings of others. Type Fours zero in on their own feelings. It's hard for them to see past the emotions swirling around inside them. But Threes actually have trouble dwelling on feelings. It's not that Threes aren't emotional. They just don't want to deal with it (how inconveniently unproductive!), so they push their emotions deep down inside.

REACT FROM THE HEART

The Feelers: Types 2, 3, 4

Struggle with shame

Long for a significant identity

THINKERS

The Thinkers are Types Five, Six, and Seven. They react primarily through mental analysis and operate from a place of anxiety or fear. But that fear shows up in different ways depending on the type.

Fives put all their energy into seeking more understanding because they're afraid they don't know enough to operate successfully in this big, scary world. Sixes internalize fear, worrying about worst-case scenarios and trying to troubleshoot every possible problem. But Sevens would rather not feel fear or anxiety. So they look outside themselves for fun and stimulation, anything to distract them from the not-so-pleasant realities of life.

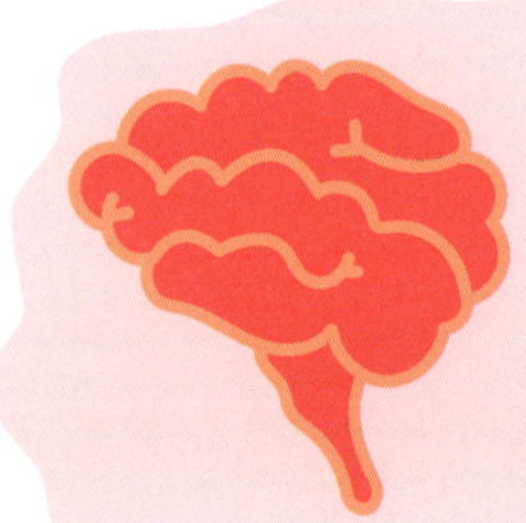

REACT FROM MENTAL ANALYSIS

The Thinkers: Types 5, 6, 7

Struggle with anxiety

Long for security

INSTINCTIVES

The Instinctives, or the gut triad, are Types One, Eight, and Nine. They have a collective longing for justice and struggle with strong feelings of anger.

Ones are uniquely in tune with how things "should" be. When they see unfairness, it brings up a surge of anger. But they quickly repress it, equating anger with being "uncontrolled and bad." This leads to a simmering resentment against themselves and others.

Eights, on the other hand, have no qualms about showing anger. They're like active volcanoes, constantly ready to erupt explosively, spewing ash and hot lava on everyone in the vicinity.

Nines are more like dormant volcanoes. They feel anger, but they don't want to disrupt the peace. So they cover it up with much more "acceptable" emotions. That doesn't mean their volcano isn't going to erupt. It just means that everyone's going to be shocked when it does.

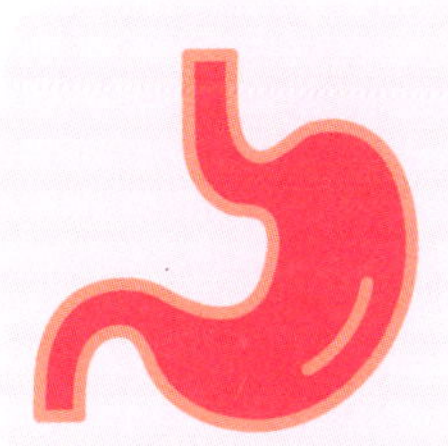

REACT FROM GUT INSTINCTS

The Instinctives: Type 1, 8, 9

Struggle with anger

Long for justice

Quiz One:

Head, Heart, or Gut?

Finding which triad you belong in will help you narrow down your type options from nine types to three. Once you figure out your triad, you will narrow your type down even further with Quiz #2.

Directions

- As you read each question, think about a recent example of when you've encountered a problem or made a decision.
- Circle the letter that best describes your answer.
- Record your answers on page 11.

Q1: When something stressful happens, which of these inner questions pops up first?

A What do I think about this?

B How do I feel about this?

C What am I going to do about this?

Q2: When you're faced with a challenge or decision, what's your first reaction?

A I immediately tune into how I or others feel about it.

B I analyze the situation and try to make sense of it before I consider emotions.

C I just know what to do—it's more of a gut reaction than something I think through.

Q3: At the end of the day, what do you really want most?

A For things to be fair and just. Don't mess with what's right!

B To know that I matter and that people see something special in me

C To feel secure—whether that's having a plan, understanding how things work, or chasing something fun so I don't have to sit in the heavy stuff

Q4: In moments of stress, I often find myself wrestling with:

A Feeling like I'm not enough

B Feeling frustrated or out of control

C Feeling worried or on edge

Q5: If you were trying to decide between two jobs, what would be the deciding factor for the job you ultimately choose?

A It's a safe choice for me—whether that safety is found in a job that allows me to live the life I want or a job that has a low risk of destabilization or fewer unknowns.

B It aligns with my values—whether it's promoting fairness, making a positive impact, standing up for social justice, or simply striving to be a good person in the world.

C It would mean I am significant—whether that be making a name for myself in my field, impressing the people around me, or being needed.

Answer Key

Q1:

A	Thinker	**B**	Feeler	**C**	Instinctive

Q2:

A	Feeler	**B**	Thinker	**C**	Instinctive

Q3:

A	Instinctive	**B**	Feeler	**C**	Thinker

Q4:

A	Feeler	**B**	Instinctive	**C**	Thinker

Q5:

A	Thinker	**B**	Instinctive	**C**	Feeler

Tally Your Answers

Using the key above, tally how many answers you recorded in each triad category. The category with the most answers is your triad!

Feeler ______
You may be a Type 2, 3, or 4.

Instinctive ______
You may be a Type 1, 8, or 9.

Thinker ______
You may be a Type 5, 6, or 7.

Core Motivations

"WHY DO YOU DO THE THINGS YOU DO?"

A common trap in your Enneagram journey is typing yourself based on external behavior. For example, the outward actions of a Nine and a Two can look very similar. They're both helpful, put others' needs before their own, and try to be kind. But if you only focus on what someone is doing, you'll miss the deeper truth: the Enneagram isn't about what you do. It's about *why* you do it. Why are you being super helpful? Why are you putting others' needs above your own? That distinction, the why behind our behavior, is the heart of the Enneagram, and we visualize it through these four categories.

CORE DESIRE

This is the thing you are constantly running toward. You're not actively thinking about it 24/7, but it's always humming in the background of your decision-making process.

CORE FEAR

This is the thing you are constantly running from, avoiding, and trying to prevent from happening.

CORE WEAKNESS

This is the core issue you are wrestling with. Another thing that sets the Enneagram apart from other personality typing systems is that instead of *just* focusing on your strengths, you are also looking at your not-so-pretty traits. The goal is to be *aware* of those weaknesses so you can manage them instead of letting them manage you.

This can also be a difficult part of your Enneagram journey; taking a deep look at your weaknesses can be unpleasant. But to be honest, it's not supposed to be a sunshine and rainbows picnic in the park. Franciscan friar and Enneagram teacher Richard Rohr wrote that "if you don't sense the whole thing as somehow humiliating, you haven't yet found your number."

SOUL MESSAGE

This is the message that your heart longs to hear. Unlike the core desire, which can be easily accessed, this is buried deep down inside you (especially if you are just beginning your self-awareness journey). It's not always the thing that you want, but it's the thing that you need.

Quiz Two:

Uncover Your Core Motivations

Directions

- Answer honestly—not how you think you should respond.
- If more than one answer fits, that's totally fine. Write down all the letters that feel like you. This quiz helps you get an array of numbers that could be your main type so you can narrow it down later.
- For each question, record the letter(s) that apply to you. (Example: C or A + F)
- Don't flip to the key yet! Wait until you've finished the quiz, then check page 22 to see which Enneagram types match your answers.

Q1: Which of these feels most uncomfortable or hard to face for you?

A Failing at something you worked hard for—and feeling like people see you as a loser

B Being blindsided by something you didn't see coming . . . and having no plan!

C Letting your guard down—then realizing someone used it against you

D Feeling stuck in a boring, repetitive routine with no room for joy or freedom

E Being thrown into a situation where you're expected to perform, but you don't feel capable, informed, or ready

F Being told you made the wrong choice—and now others are paying the price

G Realizing someone you love doesn't need you or want you in their life

H Feeling like there's nothing truly unique or special about you—that you're just like everyone else

I Being in a room full of people and feeling like no one sees or hears you

Answers: ____________________

Type (from Key): ______________

Q2: I would like my friends to describe me as . . .

A Easy to be around, thoughtful, and someone who makes others feel seen and included

B Smart, capable, and someone they can rely on to figure things out

C Deep, unique, and totally one-of-a-kind

D Someone who always does the right thing and lives by strong values

E Successful, admirable, and the kind of person who gets things done

F Loyal, trustworthy, and someone who will always have their back

G Fun, upbeat, and someone who makes life more exciting just by being around

H The most supportive and caring person they know

I Strong, honest, and unafraid to speak the truth—even when it's hard (But I don't really care how you describe me. I'm not worried about what people think.)

Answers: ____________________

Type (from Key): ______________

Q3: Hard seasons tend to shift what our personalities look like. Which of these feels most like you when you're going through a stressful time?

A I pull back and quietly stew. I start keeping score in relationships and only help if it benefits me.

B I check out completely. I keep "doing," but nothing feels meaningful—and I'm numbing more than I'd like to admit.

C I isolate completely. I stop trusting others and feel like I have to handle everything on my own.

D I get super idealistic and moody. It feels like no one understands how much I'm trying to hold everything together.

E I get overwhelmed and procrastinate. I'm distracted, unfocused, and unsure of who or what to trust.

F I get rigid and critical. I want things to go my way and get frustrated when they don't.

G I get busy to avoid spiraling. I'm anxious about everything and compare myself constantly.

H I feel overwhelmed and start chasing new ideas or distractions to avoid the anxious spiral in my head.

I I get confrontational and irritable. If people don't meet my needs, I might guilt-trip or blame them.

Answers: ____________________

Type (from Key): ______________

Q4: Which of these statements feels most true to you?

A It's important to me that I'm liked and appreciated—especially when I've gone out of my way to help.

B It's important to me to feel deeply seen and understood for who I really am.

C It's important to me to avoid pain and stay focused on what's exciting or fun.

D It's important to me to achieve big things and be recognized for my success.

E It's important to me to always be improving—I want to be a good, responsible person.

F It's important to me to feel in control of my life so no one can take advantage of me.

G It's important to me to feel capable and well-informed—I want to understand things deeply so I can rely on myself.

H It's important to me to feel at peace and keep life calm and comfortable.

I It's important to me to feel safe and supported—I want to have a plan and know I'm not alone.

Answers: ______________________

Type (from Key): ________________

Q5: What is your opinion on routines?

A There is rarely a good reason for changing up my routine. (I've perfected it!)

B Hard pass! They make me feel caged and deprived.

C Routines are my secret weapon. (Anything that boosts my productivity and helps me achieve my goals!)

D My preferred routine is often interrupted by other people's needs.

E Routine? Only if it inspires me. Otherwise, I'm too busy chasing what feels authentic.

F Following routines gives me a safety net and helps me feel ready for whatever comes my way.

G I don't need routines to get things done—I just take charge and make it happen.

H I like routines because they help me conserve my energy.

I My routines are focused around making my life as peaceful as possible.

Answers: ______________________

Type (from Key): ________________

Q6: What is your biggest fear?

A Being worthless or unsuccessful

B Being bad or corruptible

C Being ignorant or incapable

D Being alone, without any support or stability

E Being unwanted or rejected

F Being in conflict or ignored

G Being basic or boring

H Being weak or manipulated

I Being trapped or deprived

Answers: ______________________

Type (from Key): ________________

Q7: What motivates you to keep going every day?

A I want to protect myself and my loved ones.

B I want to feel peaceful in my inner and outer world.

C I want to be loved and wanted.

D I want to express my authentic self.

E I want to have security and stability in every area of life.

F I want to fulfill my responsibilities with integrity.

G I want people to see me and be impressed by what I've done.

H I want to gather all the knowledge I need to feel competent.

I I want to be happy and fully satisfied.

Answers: ______________________

Type (from Key): ________________

Q8: What's your biggest pet peeve?

A Being late . . . I hold myself to high standards, so I expect others to do the same. Be on time. It's not that hard.

B Being ignored or talked over. It makes me feel like I don't matter—and I work hard to make sure other people feel seen. So when it happens to me? Oof.

C When people reject my help or act like it doesn't matter. It's like . . . cool, guess I'll just crawl into a hole then.

D Negativity. When people constantly bring down the vibe with pain or pessimism.

E Fake people. Nothing gets under my skin more. I care deeply about being real and true to myself—so why are you pretending to be something you're not?

F When people complain about stuff they could totally fix. Like, if you hate it so much, do something. *eye roll*

G Bad leadership. Especially when someone abuses their power or doesn't own their decisions. If you're gonna be a crappy leader . . . step aside, I'll do it myself.

H Small talk. Why are we talking about the weather when we could be conserving energy like rational beings?

I Not doing what you said you'd do. If I make a commitment, I honor it. If you can't do the same? Then I don't trust you, dude.

Answers: ____________________

Type (from Key): ______________

Q9: I struggle with . . .

A Accepting negative outcomes

B Thinking of the worst-case scenario

C Analysis paralysis

D Taking care of my own needs

E Letting other people take the lead

F Feeling misunderstood

G Participating in things if I don't know enough about them

H Comparing myself to others

I Rigid and unyielding thinking

Answers: ______________________

Type (from Key): ______________

Q10: When I'm trying to get what I want or need, I tend to . . .

A Move against people. I'm gonna get my needs met, so expect me to take action, whether you like it or not.

B Move away from people. I withdraw into my inner world and try to find fulfillment alone.

C Move toward people. I'm relational, dutiful, and try to get my needs met externally.

Answers: ______________________

Type (from Key): ______________

Q11: My superpower is . . .

A Intuitively knowing what others need

B Bringing harmony to unlikely situations

C Inspiring others with my thoughts and creativity

D Mentoring others with strength and wisdom

E Making decisions based on reason and knowledge

F Troubleshooting problems when they occur

G Recovering quickly from setbacks

H Creating innovative visions for the future

I Building processes and structures that guarantee excellence

Answers: ______________________

Type (from Key): ______________

Answer Key

Q1:

A Type 3
B Type 6
C Type 8
D Type 7
E Type 5
F Type 1
G Type 2
H Type 4
I Type 9

Q2:

A Type 9
B Type 5
C Type 4
D Type 1
E Type 3
F Type 6
G Type 7
H Type 2
I Type 8

Q3:

A Type 4
B Type 3
C Type 8
D Type 1
E Type 9
F Type 7
G Type 6
H Type 5
I Type 2

Q4:

A Type 2
B Type 4
C Type 7
D Type 3
E Type 1
F Type 8
G Type 5
H Type 9
I Type 6

Q5:

A Type 1
B Type 7
C Type 3
D Type 2
E Type 4
F Type 6
G Type 8
H Type 5
I Type 9

Q6:

A Type 3
B Type 1
C Type 5
D Type 6
E Type 2
F Type 9
G Type 4
H Type 8
I Type 7

Q7:

A Type 8
B Type 9
C Type 2
D Type 4
E Type 6
F Type 1
G Type 3
H Type 5
I Type 7

Q8:

A Type 1
B Type 9
C Type 2
D Type 7
E Type 4
F Type 3
G Type 8
H Type 5
I Type 6

Q9:

A Type 7
B Type 6
C Type 9
D Type 2
E Type 8
F Type 4
G Type 5
H Type 3
I Type 1

Q10:

A You might be a Type 3, 7, or 8
B You might be a Type 4, 5, or 9
C You might be a Type 1, 2, or 6

Q11:

A Type 2
B Type 9
C Type 4
D Type 8
E Type 5
F Type 6
G Type 3
H Type 7
I Type 1

Tally Your Answers

Type 1 ________________

Type 2 ________________

Type 3 ________________

Type 4 ________________

Type 5 ________________

Type 6 ________________

Type 7 ________________

Type 8 ________________

Type 9 ________________

Putting It All Together

What were your top three types from Quiz #2 (page 15)?

____

____

____

Are any of those types in your triad?

____

____

____

Did one type show up more than other types? (Congratulations, you've found your type!)

____

____

____

If you didn't have much overlap, or you're still unsure, don't fret. These tests are only one of many ways we can find your type. Keep reading, friend!

Exercise: Words Have Power

Often we get stuck in patterns of describing ourselves. For so long, you've let your beliefs about who you are stay stagnant. I want to challenge you to wipe the slate clean. Take some time to rewrite the adjectives that describe you, helped by the people who love you best.

Adaptable
Adventurous
Affectionate
Afraid
Alert
Aloof
Ambitious
Amiable
Anxious
Arrogant
Astute
Attentive
Authentic
Aware
Awesome
Bold
Belligerent
Big-Headed
Bitter
Boastful
Bossy
Brave
Callous
Calm
Capable
Careless
Caring
Clingy
Compassionate
Confident
Confrontational
Considerate
Consistent
Courageous
Cowardly
Cruel
Cynical
Deceitful
Decisive
Defensive
Dependable
Determined
Dexterous
Diligent
Diplomatic
Domineering
Dynamic
Earnest
Encouraging
Energetic
Engaging
Enthusiastic
Fair
Fearless
Fearful
Finicky
Flexible
Flighty
Focused
Foolish
Forgiving
Forthright
Free-Spirited
Friendly
Fun-Loving
Generous
Gentle
Genuine
Giving
Greedy
Grumpy
Gullible
Happy
Hard-Hearted
Hardworking
Honest
Hopeful
Hostile
Humble
Humorous
Idealistic
Idle
Imaginative
Immature
Impolite
Indecisive
Irresponsible
Innovative
Insightful
Intolerant
Intuitive
Inventive
Joyful
Just
Kind
Loyal
Melodramatic
Menacing
Mistrustful
Moody
Motivated
Narrow-Minded
Nurturing
Observant
Open-Minded
Optimistic
Organized
Outgoing
Overcritical
Overemotional
Patient
Patronizing
People-Pleaser
Perfectionist
Persistent
Pessimistic
Playful
Pompous
Precise
Radiant
Realistic
Ruthless
Self-Centered
Selfish
Silly
Steamroller
Strong
Sullen
Thoughtless
Touchy
Untidy
Upbeat
Vain
Warm
Withholding

Ask your friends and family to text you three words that describe you.

What patterns do you see? What surprised you?

Your turn! What words would you use to describe yourself? Don't sugarcoat it; this is an important part of the process.

If any of the words make you cringe, why?

ONE & a HALF
DELVE
INTO

DEEP
THE
TYPES

Type ONE

THE REFORMER:

Moral Perfectionist, Principled Activist

"I'm hoping to do some good in the world!"

—Hermione Granger in *Harry Potter and the Deathly Hallows*, by J. K. Rowling

AT A GLANCE

Early on, Type Ones look at the world around them and hear a record scratch in their head. They do a double take, stop in their tracks, and say, "Hang on . . . things are *not* as they should be. Look at the injustice, look at the imperfection, look at *me*!"

I don't think I'm being dramatic when I say that *nobody* tries harder than Type Ones. They are not content with simply noticing that things aren't ideal. Nope, they actively reform with their thoughts, words, and actions. With their Google calendars, their physical bodies, and the way they take care of their friends and family, they feel a moral obligation to be a part of the solution.

Ones fear, more than anything, being wrong or bad. It's why they put so much emphasis on obeying the rules! However, if the common good conflicts with those rules, they will put on their "Reformer" hat and get to work.

- **CORE DESIRE:** Living with integrity and adhering to internal standards
- **CORE FEAR:** Being wrong, inappropriate, or corruptible
- **CORE WEAKNESS:** Resentment—repressing feelings and not expressing anger, leading to frustration with the self and others
- **SOUL MESSAGE:** "You are good."

CENTER OF INTELLIGENCE

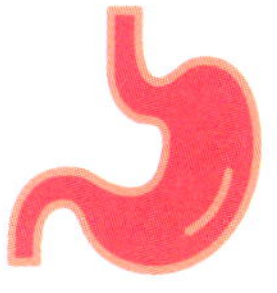

Type Ones are in the gut triad, which means they react primarily from their instincts. Ones are uniquely in tune with how things "should" be. When they see unfairness, it brings up a surge of anger. But they quickly repress it because they equate anger with being "uncontrolled." This leads to a simmering resentment against themselves and others.

TYPE ONE IRL:

Jon approached his 1,000-acre potato farm like he did his life, asking, "How can I make this better?" He set up elaborate structures with conveyor belts, trucks, and trailers to ensure everything got where it needed to go. When they started experimenting with new varieties and test plots, he crafted an elaborate system to keep everything organized. He bought the latest technology, ran the wires through the tractor and planter, and sat back, music blasting, to watch his masterpiece work. But beyond being efficient, Jon had a lot of strongly held values. He worked hard so he could hurry home to spend time with his family. And he was driven to do the right thing by his employees. He built another large barn simply so his workers would have a comfortable place to sort and load potatoes out of the elements. He ensured everyone got raises, even when times were tough. He believed fairness wasn't just a principle—it was a duty. And his work wasn't just a business to him; it reflected his integrity, a commitment to quality, and a sacred responsibility to those who depended on him.

Thinking about whether they left a lightbulb on (it's wasteful)
Slightly furrowed brow (worrying about making a mistake)
SUPPORT
Thrifted but well-kept jacket
Pin for a just cause they support
Classic wrist watch to make sure they're always on time
Upright posture (holding themselves to high standards)
Clipboard in hand (because structure and organization matter!)

What did it feel like to read the description of your main type?

Things a Type One Might Say

- "A place for everything and everything in its place."
- "You're doing it wrong."
- "That's so unfair."
- "I'll make a list."
- "Close, but no."
- "I'm not angry; just frustrated."
- "I'll just do it myself."
- "Bad planning on your part does not make an emergency on my part."
- "It's a burden being right all the time."

What strategies do you use to get your core desire?

Can you think of an instance when you struggled with your core weakness?

What does it feel like when you say your soul message out loud to yourself or have someone say it to you?

Type One IFL*: Elphaba, *Wicked*

CONSCIENTIOUS, PRINCIPLED, SELF-CRITICAL

"Some things I cannot change, but 'til I try, I'll never know."

Type Ones strive to improve themselves and the world around them, even if it costs them popularity or opportunities. This is exactly what happens when Elphaba uncovers evil power structures in Oz. Instead of enjoying a position of privilege by working with the Wizard, she defies social norms—and gravity, of course! Her strong moral compass overrides personal desires, so she devotes herself to reforming a broken system, even if it means becoming an outcast.

**In Fictional Life*

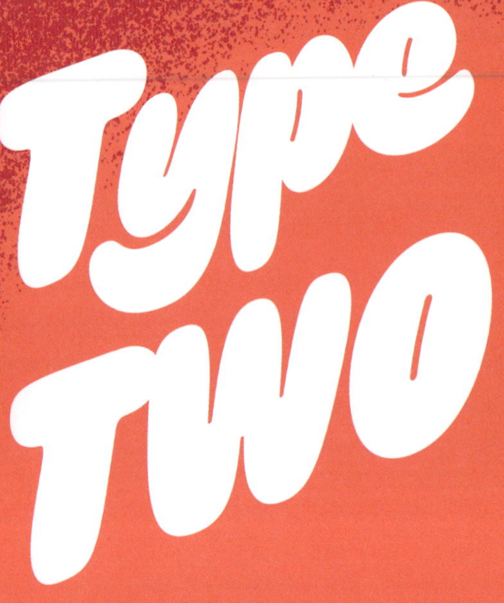

THE HELPER:

Supportive Advisor, Nurturing Warrior

"**FRODO:** Go back, Sam! I'm going to Mordor alone.

SAM: Of course you are, and I'm coming with you!"

—J.R.R. Tolkien, *The Fellowship of the Ring*

AT A GLANCE

Type Twos walk into a room and know exactly what everyone needs:

> *Lily needs a snack. Daniel needs to leave because his social battery is low. And Emily is dying for someone to ask her how her job interview went.*

Then they march in to fulfill those needs and save the day! But sometimes, this can backfire; at the end of the day, Twos are often completely drained. Not only are they suppressing their *own* needs and desires, but they give so much of themselves that now they feel resentful. "Why is no one taking care of me? How dare they take advantage of me like that!"

Underneath every Two's actions is a core fear of being unwanted. So they cope with this fear by making themselves indispensable to others.

- **CORE DESIRE:** Being appreciated, loved, and wanted
- **CORE FEAR:** Being rejected and unwanted
- **CORE WEAKNESS:** Pride—ignoring personal needs and charging forward; believing that they alone can fix everyone else's problems
- **SOUL MESSAGE:** "You are wanted and loved regardless of what you do for others."

CENTER OF INTELLIGENCE

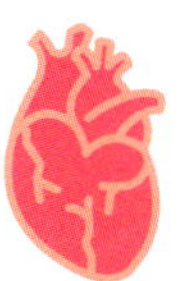

Type Twos are in the heart triad, which means they react primarily from their feelings. In the words of Selena Gomez, the heart wants what it wants! But Type Twos aren't necessarily focused on their own hearts. Rather, their laser-focused empathy is aimed at other people. How are they feeling? How can I help them?

TYPE TWO IRL:

Every time I come home after hanging out with my Type Two friend Becca, I receive some version of this text message:

I LOVED getting to see you today

Did I talk to her for two minutes after church? Go to book club with her? See her at karaoke? Yep. I'm getting a little love text. As an anxious girly, these reassurances that she enjoys our friendship make me feel so seen and wanted.

At the same time, Becca is also feeling warm and fuzzy because she's feeding her core desire: deepening connections so she can feel appreciated and loved.

But this desire has a dark side. In the pursuit of being helpful, Twos often push themselves past their breaking point. It doesn't matter if they skipped a meal or desperately need a nap—if someone needs help, they drop everything to be of service.

That's why, when Becca finally carves out a moment of peace for herself, she realizes something important: to truly love the people in her life, she has to set boundaries and practice self-care. Because as the person keeping everyone else's lives running smoothly, she needs care too.

Bags under the eyes (because they stayed up all night on the phone with a friend who needed a listening ear)
Slight head tilt to show they are actively listening
A sentimental gift from their spouse
Extra hair ties around their wrist (ready to offer one to a friend in need)
A phone in hand with multiple text notifications (keeping up multiple convos at once)
RN

Can you think of an instance when you struggled with your core weakness?

Things a Type Two Might Say

- "Are you mad at me?"
- "I'm happy to help!"
- "You're one of my favorite people."
- "I tried to help, but I think I just made it worse."
- "I'm sorry if I've been too needy lately."
- "Give yourself grace. You're doing your best!"
- "That makes my heart happy."
- "Are you okay? I noticed you haven't been your usual self today."

What did it feel like to read the description of your main type?

What strategies do you use to get your core desire?

Can you think of an instance when you struggled with your core weakness?

What does it feel like when you say your soul message out loud to yourself or have someone say it to you?

Type Two IFL*: Anna, *Frozen*

ALTRUISTIC, CHARMING, EMPATHETIC

"I'm not leaving without you, Elsa."

Twos desire love and connection above all things. So when perpetually lonely Princess Anna has the chance to marry the *so-called* man of her dreams, she jumps at the chance—despite only knowing him for, oh, five minutes. But Twos don't just seek love; they pour their hearts into giving it, often at the cost of their own well-being. Anna proves this time and time again, braving the freezing wilderness (and an angry snow monster) to find Elsa and ultimately sacrificing herself to save her sister.

**In Fictional Life*

Type THREE

THE STRIVER:

Successful Achiever, Shining Performer

"There's nothing we can't do if we work hard, never sleep, and shirk all other responsibilities in our lives."

—Leslie Knope, *Parks and Recreation*

AT A GLANCE

For Type Threes, "fail" is a four-letter word. They spend their entire lives chasing success so they won't ever have to feel the devastating consequences of failure.

Because of this, many Threes are super competitive, even with things as insignificant as playing a board game. The fear of losing sparks an intensity that might cause your family to give you a lifetime ban on playing Monopoly (not speaking from experience or anything *cough*).

This happens in some form to every single Three on the planet: they achieve something, receive positive reinforcement for that thing, and dedicate their lives to chasing that feeling. They internalize the message that their worth is dependent on their accomplishments. This is why Threes seem to accomplish goals so effortlessly.

But I want to be clear: You don't have to be a corporate ladder climber to be a Three. You'll find Threes in all walks of life: a stay-at-home parent, a post-modern sculptor, or a bird-watching aficionado. The throughline is that these types focus their superhuman efficiency on whatever objective they've decided will give them the admiration and praise they so desperately crave.

- **CORE DESIRE:** Being admired, successful, and valuable
- **CORE FEAR:** Failing at their goals and being seen as worthless and unsuccessful
- **CORE WEAKNESS:** Deceit—deceiving themselves into believing their intrinsic worth is based on their accomplishments
- **SOUL MESSAGE:** "You are valuable simply for being you and not for what you check off your to-do list."

CENTER OF INTELLIGENCE

Though Threes are part of the heart triad, it takes effort for them to feel at ease with their emotions. They often switch that part on or off depending on the version of themselves they want to present, or how much those emotions might distract from their goals.

TYPE THREE IRL:

Growing up as a scrawny little kid, Dylan was always the least athletic in his friend group. It bothered him because, as a Type Three, he tried to be the best at everything he did. In college (pre-med at UCLA), he snatches a chance at reinvention. He takes up weight training, slowly building strength, and eventually joins the rowing team—one of the lowest-ranked in the country at the time. But Dylan doesn't let minor details such as the statistical likelihood of failure get in his way. Through hard work and an unflappable go-getter attitude, Dylan becomes the team captain and helps elevate them from underdogs to "really freakin' good." So good, in fact, that the entire team is invited to help the Chinese Olympic team practice!

While all of these accomplishments sound impressive on paper (and don't get me wrong, I'm constantly impressed by Dylan's resume), it's important to note that a Three's life isn't all awards and accolades. Beneath a relentless drive to succeed lies an insidious fear—that without achievement, they are unworthy of love and approval. This constant pressure can be exhausting, often pulling Threes into the trap of toxic hustle culture. It's a relentless cycle that keeps them striving, sometimes at the cost of their own well-being.

Tousled hair that
manages to look both
attractive and like they
didn't try too hard
Holding a coffee
(helps them get
things done!)
Confident smile
ready to charm
anyone
High performance athletic gear
(to keep body in tiptop shape)
A smartwatch
to track steps,
heart rate, and an
ever-growing list of
accomplishments

What did it feel like to read the description of your main type?

Things a Type Three Might Say

- "Are you proud of me?"
- "Fake it till you make it."
- "What's your plan for today?"
- "I've had to go the bathroom for three hours, but I wanted to finish everything first."
- "Let me check my calendar."
- "I'll sleep when I'm dead."
- "Please don't interrupt me when I'm working."
- "Let's make a list."
- "Efficiency over perfection."

What strategies do you use to get your core desire?

Can you think of an instance when you struggled with your core weakness?

What does it feel like when you say your soul message out loud to yourself or have someone say it to you?

Type Three IFL*: Tiana, *The Princess and the Frog*

SUCCESS-DRIVEN, CONFIDENT, ADAPTIVE

"If you do your best each and every day, good things are sure to come your way."

Threes are driven by the need to achieve, and nobody emulates this more than Princess Tiana. She works her butt off to make her dream of owning a restaurant come true. But beyond her passion for cooking, Tiana's underlying motivation is to make her late father proud. She works endless shifts and shirks party invites, hoping her hard work will bring her closer to earning her father's admiration. But it's not until her journey through the bayou that she realizes what every Three needs to grow: True success isn't just about toughing it out and achieving something alone. It's about community, relationships, and love!

*In Fictional Life

THE INDIVIDUALIST:

Romantic Dreamer, Introspective Creative

"To be yourself in a world that is constantly trying to make you something else is the greatest accomplishment."

—Ralph Waldo Emerson

AT A GLANCE

Type Fours are often labeled "The Artist" because they can lean toward creative fields. But that creativity isn't just about art: it shapes how Fours experience the world. They notice what others overlook, feel things more intensely, and don't run from the uncomfortable.

Suffering is not scary to them. They step into it, bravely, asking, *What does this feel like? How does this affect me? How would this feel if I were someone else?* It's a raw search for authenticity.

Author Ian Morgan Cron describes being a Type Four: "If . . . you gave me the choice between going on an all-expenses-paid trip to Disney World or to the west of Ireland where I could sit atop a cliff overlooking the sea and write songs, I'd have taken Ireland in a heartbeat."

I used this Ireland example to explain Fours at a conference once. But later, a Four approached me saying, "I'd choose Disney World because of how it makes me *feel*: reconnecting with my inner child, playing make-believe, and leaning into my authentic, nerdy self."

For Fours, *feelings* are their guiding light. They inform the decisions they make, the people they trust, and the jobs that they do. For better or for worse, Fours follow their hearts from the misty Cliffs of Moher to the roller coaster of Space Mountain.

- **CORE DESIRE:** Being unique, special, and finding their authentic selves
- **CORE FEAR:** Dying without having made an impact on the world; Not being special or unique
- **CORE WEAKNESS:** Envy—feeling like they're missing a foundational and special quality that others seem to possess
- **SOUL MESSAGE:** "Your authentic self has an impact on the world."

CENTER OF INTELLIGENCE

Type Fours are in the heart triad, which means they operate largely from their emotions. I like to joke that a Four's middle name is "Feelings." They zero in on what's going on inside their own hearts, placing high importance on the outcome.

TYPE FOUR IRL:

Jillaine

Jillaine has dreamed of this moment since she was a little girl: She's in a fancy boutique wedding dress store, twirling in a princess gown with a romantic corset and big filmy fabric.

But there's a problem. She goes home with the dress . . . and cries for the next four days. She feels really silly because this stylish frock is unlike any other bride's dress and she likes being different. She didn't want to do the "typical" David's Bridal thing like the rest of her family did. But something about the boutique dress still feels wrong . . .

When she tells her therapist about it, she realizes that she built up unrealistic expectations about the whole thing, which is how she decides to let herself look for a different dress at the one place she swore she would never go: David's Bridal.

But this time she doesn't have any expectations of how she "should" feel. As she's laughing and joking with the shop assistant, it happens. She finds her dream dress. Tears fill her eyes, and she looks over to see her mom crying too. No, it's not the most original. Yes, it's from a place she had deemed too "basic." But she realized the simple process was exactly what she needed during the craziness of wedding planning.

Plus, when she married the love of her life amid the California redwoods, she didn't think once about where the dress came from—only about the joy in her heart, the love in his eyes, and the magic of the moment she'd been dreaming of all along.

JOURNAL
A single tear rolling down their cheek (not from sadness; from being overwhelmed by beauty)
A well-loved leather journal to jot down poetry that comes to mind
Wedding ring (unique, non-traditional, art-deco inspired with an ethical gemstone—less likely to be linked to conflict or human rights issues)
Barefoot (to be closer to the earth)

What did it feel like to read the description of your main type?

Things a Type Four Might Say

- "I just talked about this with my therapist."
- "My home is my sanctuary."
- "I wish it was raining."
- "You just have a certain energy."
- "When you look at the moon, do you realize Mary, Queen of Scots looked at the same moon?"
- "I'll do it when I'm in the mood."
- "How do you feel about that?"
- "Just let me be sad."

What strategies do you use to get your core desire?

Can you think of an instance when you struggled with your core weakness?

What does it feel like when you say your soul message out loud to yourself or have someone say it to you?

Type Four IFL*: Mirabel, *Encanto*

FREE-SPIRITED, HONEST, QUIRKY

"The truth is, gift or no gift, I am just as special as the rest of my family."

As the only member of her family without a magical gift, Mirabel has always felt like the odd one out—a trait found in every Four. However, what Mirabel doesn't realize is that she *does* have a gift—another trait unique to Fours: the ability to dive bravely into difficult situations! It's why Mirabel is the first in her family to recognize the cracks in Casita. Because of her bravery in confronting generational trauma, she brings healing and wholeness back to her family.

**In Fictional Life*

THE SEEKER:

Investigative Thinker, Quiet Specialist

"Nothing in life is to be feared, it is only to be understood. Now is the time to understand more, so that we may fear less."

—Marie Curie

AT A GLANCE

Fives are lifelong learners, walking through life with an insatiable curiosity. But as curious as they are about the world, they also view it as intrusive. The minute they walk out the door every morning, their energy is zapped by the expectations of people around them. So they protect themselves by gathering as much information as possible—ensuring they never have to utter the dreaded words, "I don't know."

But there's a common misconception about Fives that I want to address—Enneagram Fives as cold and distant with a monotone voice.

This essentially paints all Fives as emotionless robots. But nothing could be further from the truth! They do have emotions—they just prefer to process them privately. They're also highly selective about what personal information they share, which is why you could work with a Five for a decade and still be shocked to learn they have an identical twin or just got married.

But while Fives may be tight-lipped about their personal lives, get them talking about a topic they love and you might regret ever asking.

- **CORE DESIRE:** Being knowledgeable, capable, and competent
- **CORE FEAR:** Being useless and incapable, unable to meet expectations because of ignorance
- **CORE WEAKNESS:** Avarice—hoarding inner resources (energy, personal information, and emotions) because they feel like too much interaction with others will lead to a disastrous depletion of self
- **SOUL MESSAGE:** "Your needs are not a burden."

CENTER OF INTELLIGENCE

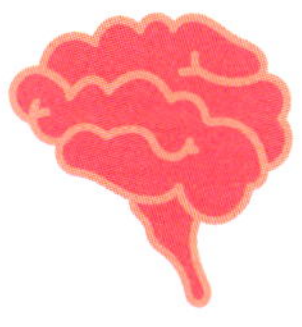

Type Fives are in the head triad, which means they react primarily from mental analysis. Because they're afraid they don't know enough to navigate this big, scary world, Fives pour their energy into seeking knowledge so they never feel incompetent.

TYPE FIVE IRL:

Charlotte

Charlotte was exploring Iceland with her friends when she stumbled upon a little town called Grindavík. But something was extremely odd about the location: It was built right on a lava field! Charlotte thought this was a weird place to build a town. And sure enough, a few months later the volcano erupted, causing a mass evacuation.

Long after she had returned home, Charlotte was still looking for answers as to why they built a town on an active volcano site. Her computer was filled with tabs showing photos, land rise stats, and volcano livestreams. In fact, during one of the livestream chats, someone mentioned that the University of Iceland was offering a free course in Icelandic volcanology. So, naturally, she signed up for the twelve-week course!

"My life is a series of rabbit holes," she later told me. "And this particular volcano happened to be one of them."

But sometimes, that thirst for knowledge backfires, leaving her feeling like she has too many tabs open in her brain. Which is something that happens to Fives when they feel overwhelmed! The mental overload makes them retreat into their inner worlds, where it's safer to observe from a distance than engage.

Reading glasses

What did it feel like to read the description of your main type?

Things a Type Five Might Say

- "Let me do a little research and get back to you."
- "I'll figure it out."
- "I know."
- "I only need four to twenty hours of alone time today."
- "I think I've peopled enough today."
- "Mornings are a no-talk zone!"
- "I'm a creature of habit."
- "Let's not and say we did."
- "I don't feel informed enough to have an opinion on that."

What strategies do you use to get your core desire?

Can you think of an instance when you struggled with your core weakness?

What does it feel like when you say your soul message out loud to yourself or have someone say it to you?

Type Five IFL*: Ross, *Friends*

CURIOUS, ANALYTICAL, INDEPENDENT

"No, Homo habilis *was erect,*
Australopithecus *was never fully erect."*

Fives often become experts in their interests, taking curiosity to the extreme—just like Ross with his dinosaur obsession. A Columbia-trained paleontologist, he geeks out about fossils and gives impressions to his students of a velociraptor's high-pitched call. Driven by curiosity, intellect, and a desire for competence, Ross relies on knowledge to give him a sense of control. But when Fives stay in observation mode too long, they risk missing out on experiencing life . . . like how it takes Ross forever to ask Rachel out!

**In Fictional Life*

THE LOYALIST:

Steadfast Guardian, Faithful Skeptic

"When I promise something, I never ever break that promise. Ever!"

—Rapunzel in *Tangled*

AT A GLANCE

Picture a Type Six as the person in the stands at a sporting event holding a giant foam finger . . . even in the pouring rain . . . even if the team is on a ten-game losing streak. They're the ride-or-die friend you've known since second grade, the coworker who always has your back.

At their core, Sixes crave security. So they spend their time making sure their stability is never in jeopardy. They do this by noticing patterns, thinking about worst-case scenarios, and troubleshooting potential problems. If you ever find yourself in a crisis, don't expect a Six to panic and say, "I don't know what to do!" Because they've already got a plan A, B, C, D . . . all the way down the alphabet.

Unfortunately, this means their minds rarely shut off, especially if they're not taking care of their stress levels. It's exhausting to be stuck in a never-ending loop of "what if this happens?"

- **CORE DESIRE:** Having security, guidance, and support
- **CORE FEAR:** Losing support and stability, be it financial, emotional, or relational
- **CORE WEAKNESS:** Anxiety—worrying about the past, present, and future; constantly anticipating worst-case scenarios
- **SOUL MESSAGE:** "All will be well."

CENTER OF INTELLIGENCE

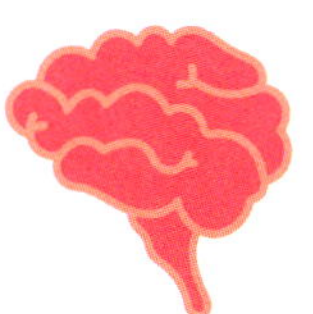

Type Sixes are in the head triad, which means they react primarily from mental analysis. But unlike the other head types, they often struggle to trust their own inner voice. That's where all that worry comes in! And while they may doubt their own judgment at times, they don't blindly follow others either. Sixes want support and guidance—but on their own terms.

TYPE SIX IRL:

David

In high school, I worked at this dinosaur science camp for kids. Sounds fancy, right? But in reality, it was just a bunch of kids digging in the sandbox for "fossils" we'd buried an hour earlier.

At the end of the summer, we got to throw a big end-of-camp bash. Even more exciting, we had a budget. So like any reasonable teenagers in charge of sixty sugar-high children, we wanted to rent the giant bouncy house shaped like a stegosaurus.

Enter David—the most responsible member of our ragtag crew and a Type Six. He practically begged us to reconsider, citing a chance of rain and the risks of an unstable, uninsured, inflatable structure. But this was Southern California—the land of eternal sunshine. We rolled our eyes, outvoted him, and went full stegosaurus.

Cut to the big day: Yep, you guessed it. Summer showers. Guess what it sounds like when those sixty kids run screaming from a giant collapsing dinosaur?

You'd think David would be gloating with an "I told you so!" But instead, the guy who gave everyone fun nicknames, memorized their food allergies, and never hesitated to stay late if a parent was running behind was busy making sure every kid was safe—because that's just who he was.

A furrowed brow (because they're running through a million contingency plans in their head)
Giant foam finger on their hand (to signify loyalty)
Umbrella strapped to their backpack (just in case)
Comfy and reliable shoes (ready for an unexpected adventure or emergency escape)

What did it feel like to read the description of your main type?

Things a Type Six Might Say

- "Just in case."
- "Not my monkey, not my circus."
- "Is it on the calendar?"
- "No worries!" (But there are, in fact, many worries.)
- "Be careful!"
- "What's the plan?"
- "Teamwork makes the dream work."
- "We should consider the worst-case scenario . . ."
- "Better safe than sorry!"

What strategies do you use to get your core desire?

Can you think of an instance when you struggled with your core weakness?

What does it feel like when you say your soul message out loud to yourself or have someone say it to you?

Type Six IFL*: Sokka, *Avatar: The Last Airbender*

TRUSTWORTHY, COURAGEOUS, RESPONSIBLE

"If I can just get out of this situation alive, I will give up meat . . . and sarcasm. Okay?"

After losing his mother and watching his father leave for war, Sokka steps up to protect his tribe, bravely shouldering the weight of responsibility as only a Type Six could. Though he has no bending powers, Sokka has a superpower that every Six possesses: a mind wired for strategy. He protects his loved ones by anticipating worst-case scenarios and crafting clever solutions. His vigilance often shows up with a dose of humor, like when he spots adorable birds in the Fire Nation and dubs them "enemy birds."

**In Fictional Life*

Type SEVEN

THE ENTHUSIAST:

Joyful Visionary, Entertaining Optimist

"Maybe other people will try to limit me but I don't limit myself."

—Jim Carrey

AT A GLANCE

Type Sevens radiate optimism, flitting from activity to activity, on the hunt for that thing that will finally fulfill them. With rose-colored glasses and a gift for spotting silver linings, they lift others' spirits and dream up innovative visions for the future with their creativity and foresight.

On the other side of all this positivity, however, is a whole lotta fear. I call it the ultimate FOMO (fear of missing out). But it's more than simply worrying about missing out on a fun weekend. Rather, it's a fear of missing out on all the goodness that life has to offer.

It's why, when bad things happen, they look on the bright side. "Bankruptcy? It's a fresh start! Jury duty? I might make new friends!"

But this life philosophy can create some big problems for Sevens. By running from all those uncomfortable feelings, they can overextend themselves with busyness . . . which eventually leads to burnout. Plus, when you're constantly focused on the next best thing, it's hard to enjoy the present moment and appreciate what you already have.

- **CORE DESIRE:** Being happy, fully satisfied, and content
- **CORE FEAR:** Being deprived and not making the most out of their time on earth
- **CORE WEAKNESS:** Gluttony—constantly seeking to be fulfilled by the next experience or stimulation
- **SOUL MESSAGE:** "You have everything you need to be happy."

CENTER OF INTELLIGENCE

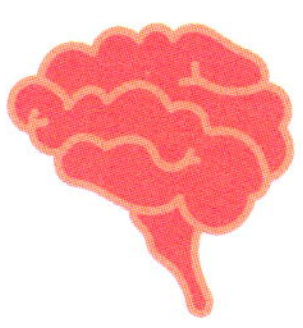

Type Sevens are in the head triad, so they respond to the world through mental analysis. For them, that often means worrying they'll end up bored or missing out. So they look outside themselves for fun and stimulation—anything to avoid the not-so-pleasant realities of life.

TYPE SEVEN IRL:

Sarina

I once asked my Type Seven friend Sarina to show me her favorite thing in her home. She then took me on a tour of photos. I hadn't realized before, but they were everywhere! On the fridge, on the wall, on a quilt!

Here's her and her dad hiking in Utah.

Here's a picture of a group hug at her sister's wedding.

Here's her mom celebrating her during her white coat ceremony for physical therapy school.

Here are her friends carving pumpkins during her annual backyard Halloween party.

As she explained the context behind each photo, her smile got wider and wider. "I just love memories!"

Knowing her warm, sweet spirit, it made sense to me that she wanted to fill her home with the faces of people she loved. Because Sarina is a connector. She loves bringing people together, forging friendships between unlikely groups of people, and creating safe spaces for beautiful memories.

A big, open-mouthed laugh (ready to crack a joke or tell a story!)
Wearing a colorful, eclectic outfit
Tons of friendship bracelets on their arm
Bag packed with snacks, a disposable camera, and a cute plushie they randomly bought
Adventure-ready shoes

What did it feel like to read the description of your main type?

Things a Type Seven Might Say

- "Anything can be fun if you make it fun."
- "The more the merrier."
- "I'll take one of each please."
- "Every cloud has a silver lining."
- "Just live and enjoy!"
- "It's going to be a great day!"
- "I can't wait for my next vacation."
- "Sorry that I wasn't myself today."
- "I SPEAK AND TEXT IN ALL CAPS!"

What strategies do you use to get your core desire?

Can you think of an instance when you struggled with your core weakness?

What does it feel like when you say your soul message out loud to yourself or have someone say it to you?

Type Seven IFL*: Lorelai, *Gilmore Girls*

ENERGETIC, CREATIVE, PLAYFUL

"There's plenty to do tonight that we can be mortified about tomorrow."

Lorelai is always chasing a Seven's core desire: freedom. From the moment she fled her strict parents' home, she was determined to live life on her own terms. She raises her daughter Rory the same way—encouraging independence, fun, and adventure. But like many Sevens, she struggles with commitment, especially in relationships (**cough** poor Max Medina). The fear of being trapped makes choosing just *one* path feel suffocating, as if choosing one thing means losing future possibilities.

**In Fictional Life*

Type EIGHT

THE PROTECTOR:

Assertive Challenger, Passionate Maverick

"I'd rather do everything for myself, and be perfectly independent."

—Jo March, *Little Women*

AT A GLANCE

When they were young, Eights experienced some form of betrayal. That feeling was so jarring and uncomfortable that they vowed to never be that vulnerable again. So Eights spend their lives making sure they're always protected. They extend that protection to the people in their lives as well. I know an Eight who saved her entire team from layoffs during the pandemic. She went to bat for each and every person, and they loved and respected her for it.

That's why Eights often rise to positions of power. They're leaders, changemakers, activists, and bosses—invigorated by obstacles rather than intimidated by them. This fierce drive is what makes them so effective at achieving goals and getting things done.

But the same traits that can make Eights incredible mentors and protectors can also backfire. Especially when their fear of being betrayed makes them avoid vulnerability at all costs. Their personal motto becomes "it's my way or the highway." They don't listen, they steamroll, and their big, loving hearts become heavily guarded behind barbed wire and crocodile-filled moats.

- **CORE DESIRE:** Protecting yourself and your loved ones
- **CORE FEAR:** Being weak, powerless, or manipulated
- **CORE WEAKNESS:** Excess/Lust—constantly desiring intensity, control, and power; steamrolling others to get what they want
- **SOUL MESSAGE:** "You will not be betrayed."

CENTER OF INTELLIGENCE

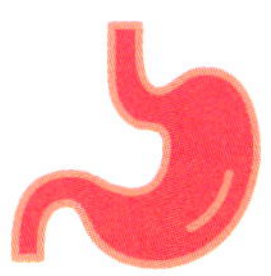

Type Eights are in the gut triad, which means they react primarily from their instincts. They respond to injustice quickly and instinctively. It's very much act first, think later. Their primary goal is to protect themselves and others from being harmed.

TYPE EIGHT IRL:

When Stacey started her job as the executive director of the Kansas African American Affairs Commission, she immediately thought, *This is the perfect job for an Enneagram Eight.* For the first time in her life, she was surrounded by people who made decisions as quickly as she did. It was exhilarating—a work environment that matched her natural pace of *fire, aim, ready.*

But the intensity came at a cost, especially when she was running for state senate—for the second time—while balancing her full-time job. One late Friday night, after hours of making calls to voters, she was strategizing with her deputy chief of staff and a realization hit her: *This is not sustainable. I love my work, but if I don't set boundaries, I'm going to burn out.*

This struggle is common for Eights, particularly when their work revolves around injustice. They see problems and think, *If no one else is stepping up to fix this, then it's my responsibility.*

For Stacey, that sense of duty is strongest when people she cares about are being mistreated. "I will punch you in the eye," she once said, "if I see you hurt someone I care about." But as fiercely as she protects others, it's easy for her to forget to protect something just as important—her own time, boundaries, and self-care.

Confident power stance

Tailored suit (to give off "I've got this" vibes)

Glasses (to better spot injustice)

Classic gold hoop earrings that belonged to their grandmother (a tribute to the strong women who came before them)

Campaign button

Sturdy shoes (ready for action and to stand their ground if needed!)

What did it feel like to read the description of your main type?

Things a Type Eight Might Say

- "Let the bridges I burn light the way."
- "Please wait till I've had my coffee."
- "If I felt that way, I would've told you."
- "Not my problem."
- "Don't you dare apologize if you're not in the wrong."
- "Rules are suggestions."
- "Just do it or quit talking about it."
- "Fire, aim, ready!"
- "That seems like a 'you' problem."
- "I've got your back."

What strategies do you use to get your core desire?

Can you think of an instance when you struggled with your core weakness?

What does it feel like when you say your soul message out loud to yourself or have someone say it to you?

Type Eight IFL*: Furiosa, *Mad Max: Fury Road*

STRONG, PROTECTIVE, RESILIENT

"Out here, everything hurts. You wanna get through this? Do as I say. Now pick up what you can and run."

No one tells Furiosa what to do. Sound familiar, Eights? When Immortan Joe's wives are threatened, she doesn't hesitate to step in as their protector, even when the odds are stacked against her. That's the essence of Eights: fiercely defending themselves and those they love, no matter the cost. Ultimately, by overthrowing the dictator and reclaiming the Citadel, Furiosa's protection extends to all the oppressed people under Joe's rule; there's nothing Eights hate more than an unjust leader who tries to control them.

**In Fictional Life*

THE PEACEMAKER:

Peaceful Mediator, Adaptive Diplomat

"You can't stay in your corner of the Forest waiting for others to come to you. You have to go to them sometimes."

—*Winnie-the-Pooh*, by A. A. Milne

AT A GLANCE

Enneagram Nines often have a difficult time discovering their main type. Because their whole lives they've worked very hard at blending in, merging with others, and putting themselves into other people's shoes. It's what makes them such great mediators and diplomats! Usually, they've been practicing this since childhood, like being a peacemaker between two bickering siblings.

But this love of peace comes at a cost. By always going with the flow, Nines miss out on a crucial thing: themselves. They push down their passions and needs, falling asleep to who they really are. The fear behind this is that, if they assert themselves, they will lose connection with others.

But all this suppression does is make Nines a dormant volcano. When they feel ignored or devalued, anger bubbles like lava beneath the surface. They try to cover this anger with more *acceptable* emotions. But make no mistake, that volcano will inevitably erupt, and it will usually be at a random time, leaving everyone—including the Nine—shocked and saying, "Where did that come from?"

- **CORE DESIRE:** Having inner stability and peace of mind
- **CORE FEAR:** Being in conflict; losing connection with others; being ignored
- **CORE WEAKNESS:** Complacency—falling asleep to inner passions and desires to keep the peace; refusing to acknowledge anger
- **SOUL MESSAGE:** "Your voice matters."

CENTER OF INTELLIGENCE

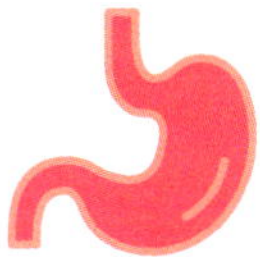

Type Nines are in the gut triad, which means they react primarily from their instincts. But instead of acting on those instincts, they suppress them. They don't want their assertions to lead to conflict.

TYPE NINE IRL:

Matt was sick of living for other people. Everything was suffering: his work, his relationship to his daughters, and even his physical health! But every time he tried to prioritize himself, other people's needs got in the way. It wasn't until his daughter, a Type Five and Enneagram fan, started sending him Instagram posts about Type Nines that Matt realized he wasn't the only one who struggled with this. For the first time, he didn't feel alone!

"Dad," his daughter said after sending one particularly poignant Type Nine post. "If you want to be happier, you need to learn boundaries."

So the next day, Matt gave it a shot. He had been wrestling with a problem (silently, of course) for years. Every single morning of their marriage, Matt's wife woke up and—before she even got out of bed—checked the news. When natural disasters devastated a city or a beloved celebrity died, his wife would launch into a conversation about it with him.

But today, he wanted things to be different. So before she had a chance to describe the latest economic downturn, Matt said, "Hey, I don't like to start off the day with bad news. I internalize it, and it makes my day horrible."

What happened next shocked him: She honored his boundary. He realized that asking for what he wanted actually worked. And it made a *huge* difference! Now instead of letting the overwhelm of the world dump on him first thing in the morning, he sticks to a calm routine that sets him up for a more peaceful day.

Slightly messy hair (just woke up from a nap)
Steaming cup of tea
Casual and approachable stance
Oversized hoodie ('cause cozy is king)
Animals LOVE their energy
Leather bracelet engraved with a peace sign

What did it feel like to read the description of your main type?

Things a Type Nine Might Say

- “No worries! It’s fine!”
- “All will be well.”
- “Sorry to bother you!”
- “People need to care about each other.”
- “You decide.”
- “Do you want a little treat?”
- “I just need to lay down fo a bit.”
- “Does that make sense?”
- *sigh*

What strategies do you use to get your core desire?

Can you think of an instance when you struggled with your core weakness?

What does it feel like when you say your soul message out loud to yourself or have someone say it to you?

Type Nine IFL*: Luke Skywalker, *Star Wars*

EASYGOING, ACCEPTING, COMPASSIONATE

"I'll never turn to the dark side . . . I'm a Jedi, like my father before me."

Throughout his hero's journey, Luke, a classic Nine, seeks peace—both within himself (Jedi path or Dark Side?) and in the chaotic world around him. When he refuses to kill Darth Vader, his compassion is what ultimately leads to the resolution of a broader conflict. Like many Nines, Luke also struggles with withdrawal and passivity: he stays on his uncle's farm despite hating it and later exiles himself out of shame after failing his students and losing Ben Solo to the dark side. These moments reveal his tendency to retreat from emotional turmoil, torn between action and avoidance.

*In Fictional Life

THIS OR THAT: THE DIFFERENCE BETWEEN SOME SIMILAR TYPES

To understand the difference between two common types with some overlap, ask yourself which of these statements is more true to you. If a type pairing is not here, it doesn't mean that it can't be mistyped; it's just not seen as often.

Type 1 or Type 2?

1 I do good things to be seen as a good person.

2 I do good things to gain validation from others.

Type 1 or Type 3?

1 I work hard so I can achieve perfection in all things.

3 I work hard so I can prove that I'm worthy of love and admiration.

Type 1 or Type 6?

1 I have an inner critic who is constantly criticizing me.

6 I have an inner chorus of voices constantly filling my head with worry and anxiety.

Type 1 or Type 8?

1 When I'm angry, I implode.

8 When I'm angry, I explode.

Type 1 or Type 9?

1 I get upset with myself when I'm not behaving up to my moral or ethical standards.

9 I get upset with myself when I don't make others happy.

Type 2 or Type 6?

2 When asked for advice, I give my opinion freely.

6 When asked for advice, I feel some self-doubt about my response.

Type 2 or Type 7?

2 I have trouble balancing my own desires with other people's.

7 I don't have an issue satisfying my own desires.

Type 2 or Type 8?

2 My greatest fear is being rejected and unloved.

8 My greatest fear is being harmed and betrayed.

Type 2 or Type 9?

2 I insert myself into others' lives to help them because I know what's best for them.

9 I help others only when they ask for my help, and bonus: it reduces the potential for conflict.

Type 3 or Type 7?

3 I don't like quitting anything because I avoid feeling failure at all costs.

7 I don't mind switching up my goals because I can just reframe it into something positive!

Type 3 or Type 8?

3 I will adjust how I am perceived so I can be liked.

8 I won't change who I am to be liked.

Type 3 or Type 9?

3 I work hard, and my personal goals take priority over most things.

9 I work hard, but my personal goals can be waylaid by other people's needs.

Type 4 or Type 5?

4 My emotions help me navigate difficult situations.

5 I prefer to detach from my feelings when difficult situations arise.

Type 4 or Type 8?

4 Vulnerability makes me feel understood.

8 Vulnerability makes me feel weak.

Type 5 or Type 6?

5 At the end of the day, I can only trust my own mind.

6 I'm not always confident in my own mind so I look for trust outside of myself.

Type 6 or Type 8?

(This does not apply to a Counterphobic Type Six. See further reading section on page 205 for more information about subtypes.)

6 I want to win the approval of those in authority (even if I don't like them).

8 I want to be the authority (especially if I don't like the current leaders).

Type 6 or Type 9?

6 I think about bad things that might happen so I can troubleshoot them.

9 I prefer not to think about things that might upset me.

Type 7 or Type 8?

7 More than anything, I want to feel happy and satisfied.

8 More than anything, I want to protect myself and my loved ones.

Type 7 or Type 9?

7 I know what I want!

9 I have trouble knowing what I want.

Now, That's My Type!

TWO
STEP
THE

STRESS
BURNOUT
CYCLE

“I say, if your knees aren’t green by the end of the day you ought to seriously re-examine your life.”

—CALVIN IN *CALVIN AND HOBBES*,
BY BILL WATTERSON

THE ENNEAGRAM ARROWS

Picture your personality during the most stressful time of your life. Then, picture it again during one of your happiest moments. They look different, but they're both *you*.

This is something that sets the Enneagram apart from other typing systems: It acknowledges that your personality isn't set in stone. And thank goodness for that! I certainly don't want to go through life with the same personality that I had in my twenties, dating toxic people and being totally insecure (RIP).

As I age, I want to grow and mature! I want my inner monologue to be wise and kind, my hard edges to be smoothed out, my blind spots out in the open.

The wonderful news is we have a tool to help us do that! It's called the Enneagram Arrows. On the Enneagram symbol, each type has two lines connecting it to two other types. These lines, or arrows, show the relationship your main type has with those connecting numbers.

Your stress arrow shows where you go when you're in a negative place or super stressed out. This is a warning sign that something is not okay. For example, when they're stressed, Type Ones go to the unhealthy side of Type Four. That doesn't mean they've suddenly become a Four. It simply means they start behaving like a struggling Four, submitting to "woe is me" feelings and withdrawing from other people.

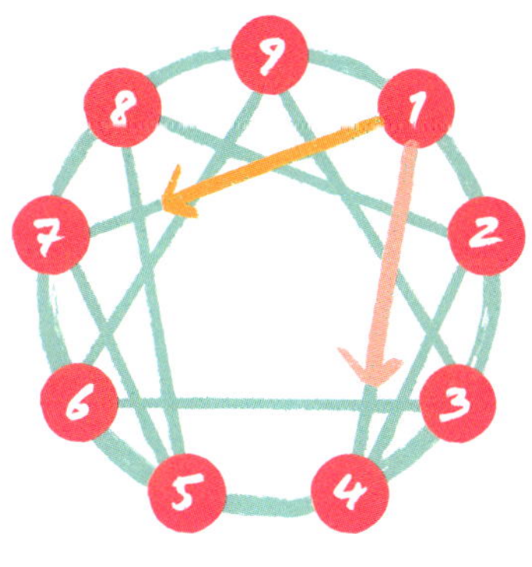

YOUR STRESS ARROW

YOUR GROWTH ARROW

When you notice that you're leaning into your stress arrow, it's a chance to check in with yourself: "What needs to change?"

Then, your growth arrow helps you answer that question by showing you where you go when you feel safe, secure, and healthy. For example, Type Ones go to the healthy side of a Type Seven. This looks like pulling from the higher levels of Type Seven to embrace the lighter side of life.

In this next section, you will learn about the warning signs that signal when each type is veering into its stress path. Then discover the action steps you can take to pull yourself into a growth path!

TYPE ONE ARROWS

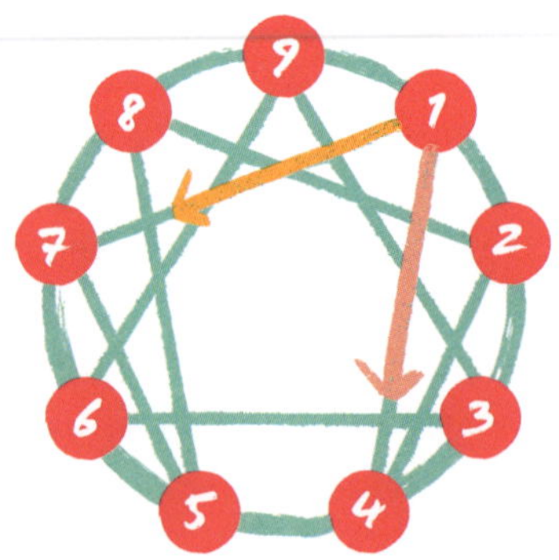

YOUR STRESS ARROW
Average to unhealthy side of Type 4

YOUR GROWTH ARROW
Healthy side of Type 7

WARNING SIGNS: You feel resentful about unfulfilled expectations and long for an idyllic world where everything is perfectly up to your standards. You sink into depression and want to run away from all your problems. You feel deeply misunderstood by everyone in your life.

HOW TO GROW: Embrace your inner child! Try out something creative and new, even if you aren't good at it. Do your very best to release the need for perfection. Laugh often and find joy in your daily life.

TYPE TWO ARROWS

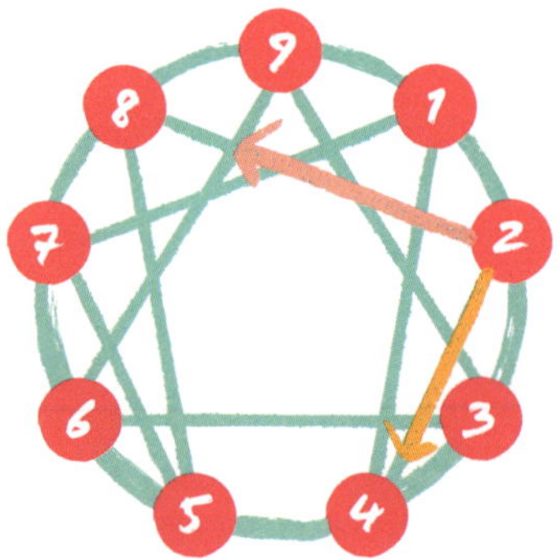

YOUR STRESS ARROW
Average to unhealthy side of Type 8

YOUR GROWTH ARROW
Healthy side of Type 4

WARNING SIGNS: You feel very confrontational and irritable. You manipulate other people if you feel like your needs aren't being met. You blame others for what's going wrong. Angry outbursts are more common.

HOW TO GROW: Stop and think: "*Why am I helping this person?*" and "*What am I feeling and wanting right now?*" Prioritize your self-care by saying no and maintaining those boundaries. Let yourself feel anger, sadness, and all those tricky emotions you usually run from.

TYPE THREE ARROWS

WARNING SIGNS: You totally shut down and numb out through things like TV, food, or video games. You remain busy, but you aren't doing anything of substance. You lose interest in things that used to bring you joy.

HOW TO GROW: Open up about your challenges to your community, even if you feel embarrassed by what you're struggling with. By letting yourself be vulnerable, you're providing space for others to step in and support you. You don't need to have it all together.

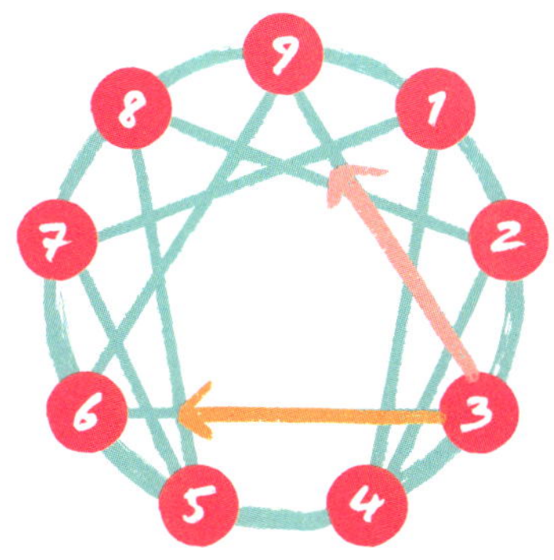

YOUR STRESS ARROW
Average to unhealthy side of Type 9

YOUR GROWTH ARROW
Healthy side of Type 6

TYPE FOUR ARROWS

WARNING SIGNS: You punish others by withdrawing your help and friendship while simultaneously feeling insecure about the status of those relationships. You start to only do things for others if there are strings attached.

HOW TO GROW: Create structure in your life so you can act on all those beautiful ideas you have. Practice gratitude so you can stay present and thankful. This will help you stay grounded and balanced.

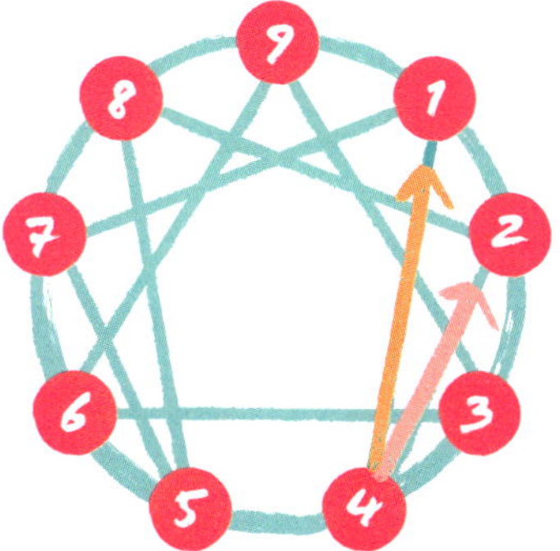

YOUR STRESS ARROW
Average to unhealthy side of Type 2

YOUR GROWTH ARROW
Healthy side of Type 1

TYPE FIVE ARROWS

WARNING SIGNS: Your mind is on overdrive and focus feels impossible. You chase new ideas to escape the anxiety, make impulsive decisions, and overload your plate with tasks you hope will quiet the noise in your head.

HOW TO GROW: Get active! Exercise your brain *and* your body. Start saying yes. You will find growth and health when you participate instead of just observe.

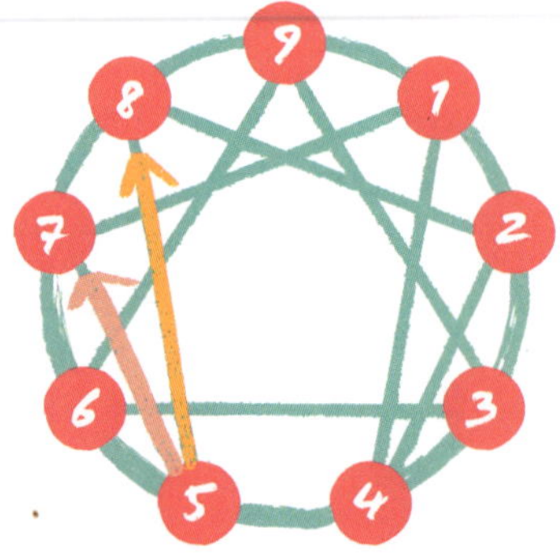

YOUR STRESS ARROW
Average to unhealthy side of Type 7

YOUR GROWTH ARROW
Healthy side of Type 8

TYPE SIX ARROWS

WARNING SIGNS: You keep busy to avoid addressing your anxiety. You stress about your image and overanalyze interactions with others. You start comparing yourself to others, which makes you feel both insecure and competitive.

HOW TO GROW: Take a deep breath, slow your mind, and relax. Prioritize taking care of yourself, and not just by indulging in a spa weekend. Nurture the parts of your soul that need refreshment and encouragement as well.

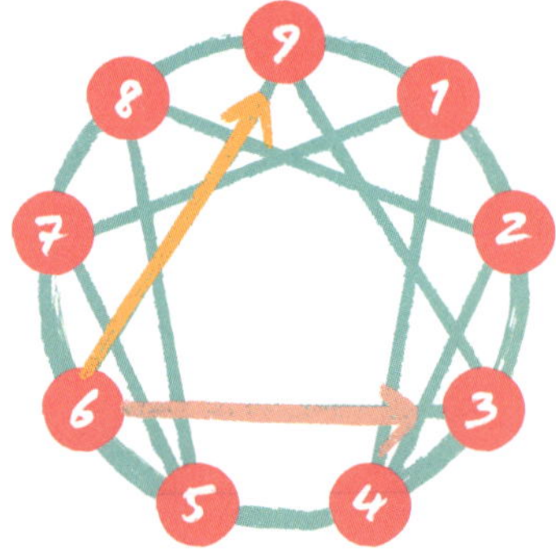

YOUR STRESS ARROW
Average to unhealthy side of Type 3

YOUR GROWTH ARROW
Healthy side of Type 9

TYPE SEVEN ARROWS

WARNING SIGNS: You build up walls and rules. You are more critical of yourself and others. Your inner perfectionist comes out in full force. You get upset with people when they mess up your fun plans.

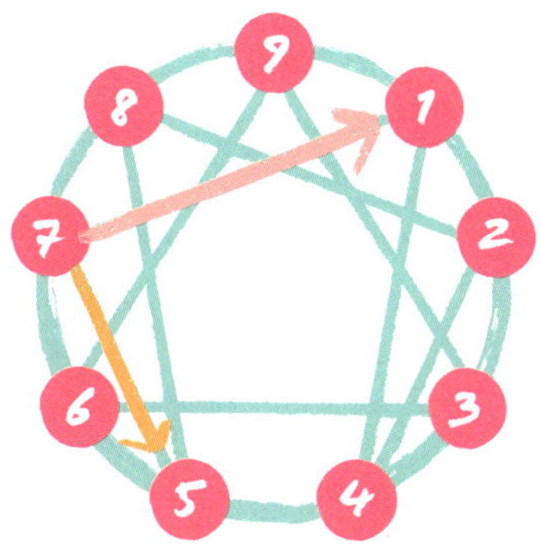

YOUR STRESS ARROW
Average to unhealthy side of Type 1

YOUR GROWTH ARROW
Healthy side of Type 5

HOW TO GROW: Don't try to distract yourself from hard emotions and situations. Take time to slow down and research things you care about. Build intentional rest into your daily routine, leaning into the groundedness of Type Fives.

TYPE EIGHT ARROWS

WARNING SIGNS: You withdraw and detach from the world, refusing to ask for help. You are less action-oriented, withdrawing into your inner world. You distrust others and feel like you can only rely on yourself.

YOUR STRESS ARROW
Average to unhealthy side of Type 5

YOUR GROWTH ARROW
Healthy side of Type 2

HOW TO GROW: Be a positive force in other people's lives. Stand up for others even if it doesn't serve your own needs. Allow yourself to share uncomfortable feelings with the people you love and trust. It's also helpful for you to get back into your body through movement.

TYPE NINE ARROWS

WARNING SIGNS: You are anxious and constantly thinking about worst-case scenarios. You procrastinate on your responsibilities and struggle with staying focused and present. You struggle to trust yourself and others.

YOUR STRESS ARROW
Average to unhealthy side of Type 6

YOUR GROWTH ARROW
Healthy side of Type 3

HOW TO GROW: Take time to *actually* think about what you want and how you want to achieve it. You have the ability to tap into a Three's proactive nature and achieve your goals. Speak up when you feel like your voice isn't being heard.

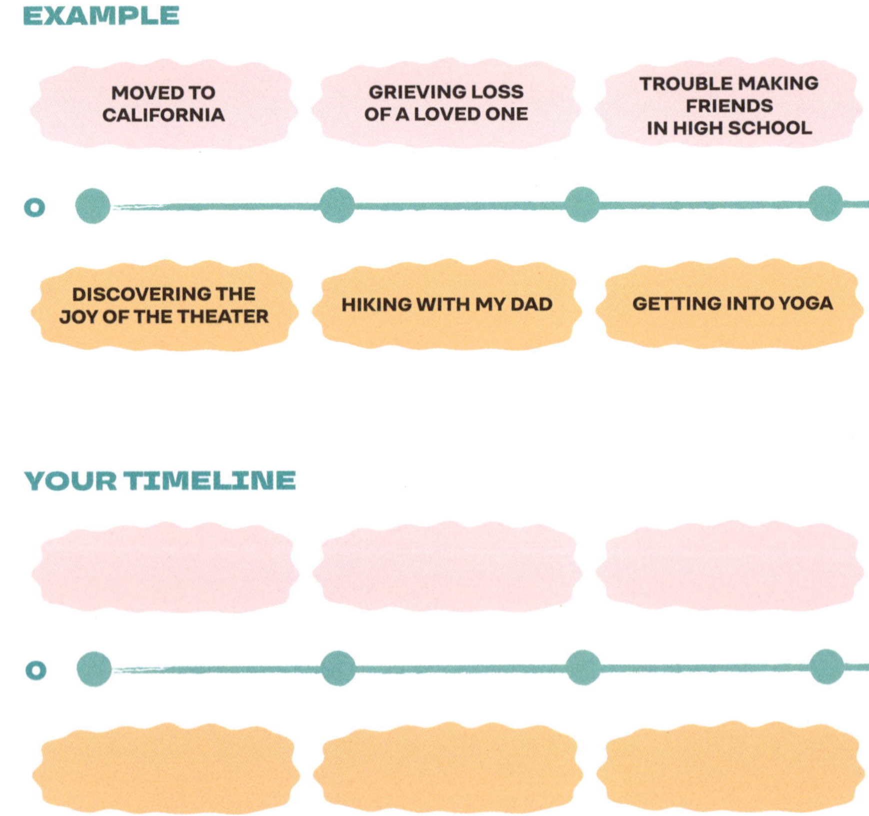

EXERCISE: THE STRESS AND REST TIMELINE OF YOUR LIFE

Write your current age at the end of the timeline.

Think about the negative, upsetting moments in your life. Fill them into the "stressful" blocks starting from childhood to your current age.

Do the same for the "restful" blocks, instead thinking about the most restful, positive moments in your life.

See my own timeline as an example.

What life events contributed to your most stressful moments?

At these low points, what did you do to help yourself feel better?

Do you see any themes or patterns in your rest blocks? (For example, my restful moments involve being active and finding community.)

Do you see any themes or patterns in your stress blocks? (For example, my stressful moments revolve around instability and loneliness.)

What life events contributed to your most restful moments?

What can you do to create more restful moments in your life?

Burnout

Nothing zaps the joy out of life quite like burnout. But sometimes you don't even know you're headed into dangerous waters until it's too late. Especially because burnout looks so different for each Enneagram type. Take a look at these warning signs to see what you need to watch out for.

1 Resentful, sick, perfectionism on overdrive

2 Aggressive, irritable, demanding of others

3 Apathetic, using numbing tactics like food or TV

4 Simultaneously want to be alone and want others to emphathize

5 Overbooking, impulsive decisions, impatience

6 Stressed, trouble sleeping, hard to breathe deeply

7 Self-critical, missing sense of joy, bogged down

8 Withdrawn, preferring to observe rather than participate, distrustful

9 Masking your needs, forgetful, inability to rest

BURNOUT PREVENTION TIPS

Type One

It's common for you to ignore the signs of burnout completely. You'll work yourself past your breaking point, then be super confused when your body decides to take a break *for* you. This usually looks like extreme fatigue or illness. The key to fixing this is to rest *before* your body forces you to slow down. I had a therapist who once said, "If you don't schedule a break, your body will take one for you. And it probably won't be at a convenient time!" So schedule intentional breaks into your daily, weekly, and quarterly plans.

Type Two

Create healthy boundaries . . . and stick to them. First, ensure you have a clearly defined list of things that are okay and not okay. Then, when your boundaries are in danger of being crossed, say no. I know that's easier said than done, but I have a little tip to help you accept this discomfort. Tell yourself: "I have a right to say no. I have a right to take care of myself." Plus, it's not always going to feel so awkward. With time and practice, it becomes easier and easier.

Type Three

You need an activity that gets you out of your head and into your body so you can be fully present. This could be regular hikes, yoga, or a tap dancing class. Whatever joyful movement makes you happy! But beyond activity, you also need to confide in someone about how you're feeling. This can feel super embarrassing because you might not want to admit that you're not the productive superhero you present to the world. But if you want to beat burnout, you must tell someone you're hurting. By speaking it into existence, you're making it real for yourself and asking for accountability to help you get out of your rut.

Type Four

Whether or not you consider yourself an artist, all Fours need to incorporate creativity into their daily lives. Without it burnout is inevitable. Your soul needs to connect with something deeper, something beautiful, especially when your daily life feels monotonous and difficult. What brings you joy? What brought you joy when you were a child? What is something creative that you can do just for the fun of it?

Type Five

Cut back on your commitments. Make a list of everything that needs to be done. If it's non-negotiable, can it be delegated? If it doesn't need to be done, get rid of it. Simplify your calendar, clean your home (or hire someone to do it for you), and give yourself space to *breathe* so you can enjoy your life.

Type Six

Create a mind map for what you're feeling. Start by writing a feeling or thought in the middle of a piece of paper. Then, draw a circle around it. From there, write more feelings and thoughts that come up, using branches and circles to connect them. This will help you take the confusing jumble of thoughts out of your mind and turn them into something tangible. If that feels too overwhelming, just write "curing my burnout" on a blank piece of paper. Then, brain dump every coping skill that comes to mind.

Type Seven

I asked Sarajane Case, author of *The Honest Enneagram* and a Type Seven, to weigh in on this. She's a fantastic Enneagram resource (seriously, go read her book) and a highly productive creative who has experienced burnout firsthand. She said, "I have to cut out everything that isn't urgent and do something spontaneous. I also meditate daily, watch sad movies so I can cry, brain dump all of the things on my mind, and recommit to my top priorities so I can focus on what's important instead of everything else I think sounds fun but is actually stressful."

Type Eight

Have you stopped moving your body? This is a huge clue for Eights that your check engine light is on. Because Eights operate with such passion and intensity, you need to have a physical outlet to complete the stress cycle. In their book *Burnout: The Secret to Unlocking the Stress Cycle*, Drs. Amelia and Emily Nagoski write that exercise is "your first line of attack in the battle against burnout." An Eight friend of mine does Olympic weightlifting after work because she finds it's the only time her mind quiets. But if you're an exercise-skeptic like another Eight I know, try tricking yourself into moving with a few laps around the mall or attend an ABBA dance party.

Type Nine

You may feel anxious and have trouble waking up in the morning. You may be masking your needs and taking care of everyone but yourself. You may feel like there's something really important that you need to do, but you just can't remember what it is! That's burnout, sweet Nines. To cure this, you need to gain clarity about what you truly want in life. Ask your therapist to help you do this or start meeting with a friend (may I suggest a Type 1 or Type 3?) to be your accountability partner.

Seven Science-Backed Ideas to Fight Burnout

According to Drs. Amelia and Emily Nagoski, you can decrease burnout stressors by:

- Moving your body
- Laughing
- Breathing exercises
- Crying
- Having a deep chat with a loved one
- Doing something creative
- Engaging in casual and friendly interactions

EXERCISE: BUILD YOUR BURNOUT TOOL KIT

Think about the warning signs that tell you burnout is coming. What unsuccessful ways have you tried to prevent burnout?

EXERCISE

Burnout Took Kit Example

1. Fill in your stressors—these are warning signs before burnout.
2. What are your ideas to help alleviate them? See page 119 for more ideas if needed.
3. Pick an idea and make it into an actionable task you can achieve within a week.

EXAMPLE

STRESSORS	I can't relax in my home. The street noise and neighbors are so loud.	I have so many pent up emotions in me and I don't know what to do.	I feel so alone.
IDEAS	Create a quiet space for relaxing at the end of the day.	Journal my thoughts and feelings.	Have a casual and friendly social interaction.
STRATEGY	Get a white noise machine. Ask the neighbor to stop the loud music during the hours of 7–9 p.m. (bring them brownies to sweeten the deal).	Put 20 minutes of journaling into my calendar. Honor that time. Write whatever comes to mind.	Go read at a coffee shop and strike up a brief conversation with a barista. Ideas: How's your day going? Has it been busy today? I'm new to the area, any suggestions for lunch?

STRATEGY	IDEAS	STRESSORS

THE RIGHT KIND OF REST

We've all internalized the words of the great philosopher Kelly Clarkson: "What doesn't kill you makes you stronger." But the truth is, what doesn't kill you makes you so freaking tired. That's why the best thing you can do when burnout hits is *rest*. I found this out firsthand when I quit YouTube for a month. I spent my free time exploring my city with my husband, walking my corgi, Lemon, and going on hikes. The result? I went from wanting to quit YouTube *forever* to having tons of new ideas and excitement to create again.

But not all forms of rest actually help you. If you've ever spent hours in bed binging Netflix only to feel even *more* disheartened afterward, you know what I mean. There's a difference between numbing rest and restorative rest! Don't get me wrong—numbing rest isn't always a bad thing; I certainly need my fair share of eating Hot Cheetos and playing *Animal Crossing*. But if you really want to get yourself out of a burnout state, your rest needs to be more active and intentional. Here are some examples:

Numbing Rest	Restorative Rest
Binging TV	Going for a walk in nature
Scrolling on social media	Listening to music
Playing video games for hours	Building something
Unhealthy snacking	Yoga
Online shopping	Conversation with a loved one
Gossiping about people	Talking about ideas
Drinking alcohol	Writing a short story

In the left column, write rest activities that temporarily numb you but don't necessarily have a meaningful impact on your overall state of being.

In the right column, write rest activities that make you feel alive and refreshed.

Numbing Rest	Restorative Rest

When was the last time you did something that counts as restorative rest?

Did you feel guilty about carving that time out for yourself?

Where does that guilt come from?

What excuses do you give yourself to *not* rest?

Parent yourself! If you said those excuses as a small child, what would you want an adult to say to you?

Sketch out what your next three days look like. Can you find a restorative restful activity?

Pockets of Peace

A pocket of peace is a time in your day when you experience a moment of stillness, a feeling of gratitude, or a breath of fresh air. Once you notice a pocket of peace, pay attention! This is the universe giving you a gift of tranquility amid the overwhelm. Honor yourself and give it a moment to fill you with calm.

I asked Enneagram types on my Instagram to share their pockets of peace. I was expecting to get a *lot* of different answers (and don't get me wrong—everyone has their own version!), but I did find some common themes within each type.

PEACE THEMES FOR YOUR TYPE:

Type 1: self-care

Type 2: warmth

Type 3: authenticity

Type 4: creativity

Type 5: solitude

Type 6: stillness

Type 7: freedom

Type 8: satisfaction

Type 9: presence

TYPE ONE

Organizing mess into manageable lists

Cooking a healthy, delicious dinner

Early mornings with an empty inbox and coffee

TYPE TWO

An outdoor summer BBQ

Gathering with all the people I love

Sunrises (and new beginnings)

TYPE THREE

Time with a loved one, who can peel away the layers

When someone tells me they are proud of me

TYPE FOUR

Nothing on my to do list

Staring at the moon and thinking of all the people who are also gazing at it

A good cry

TYPE FIVE

Solo walk through the farmer's market

Staring at the night sky thinking about how small we are

Reading a book

TYPE SIX

Planning things I enjoy

Meditation

Long drives with an open sunroof

TYPE SEVEN

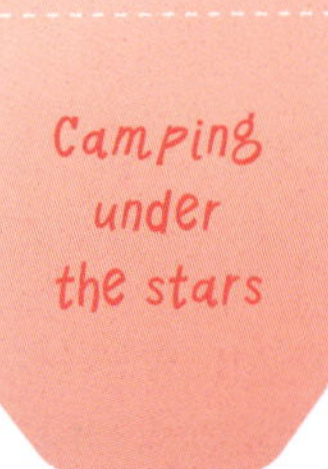

TYPE EIGHT

Hiking in a beautiful place

Costco pizza after a successful grocery run

Knowing everything is in order

TYPE NINE

Lookout views from mountain tops

A summer dinner party with friends and family

Stillness in the sunshine

What did not ring true for you in this section? Write it down and leave it in this workbook. No need to carry anything that isn't helpful for your journey!

How have you attempted to handle stress in the past?

What tools would you like to use from this section to help you in the future?

THREE
GREW
YOUR

into
BEST
SELF

"Don't get so busy making a living that you forget to make a life."

—DOLLY PARTON

WARNING:
CRINGINESS AHEAD

This is the point in your workbook journey that is going to make you cringe. I know, I know. Why invite that into your life? But please hear me out! I promise it's going to be worth it. The Enneagram is only valuable if it leads to positive change in your life. Otherwise, it's just another fun fact at a cocktail hour. This section is here to help you create that change by offering tips, tools, and exercises to achieve your goals. You'll uncover your type's core struggles, learn how to overcome them, and explore your Enneagram wings for a deeper understanding of what makes you *you*.

Overcoming Your Core Weakness

This is the big elephant in the room, ugh-do-we-have-to-talk-about-this issue for your type: your core weakness.

It's what's holding you back from living out your deepest purpose, stopping you from feeling aligned, and keeping you stuck in standstill traffic on a one-lane highway.

The good news is that once you're aware of your core weakness, you can work on it, get the tow trucks in, and clear out your path! And that's the main goal of the Enneagram: managing your weakness rather than letting it manage you.

ONE

RESENTMENT—Repressing feelings and not expressing anger, leading to frustration with yourself and others

Type Ones are motivated by a strong sense of right and wrong. When they see people acting out in anger, they see that as a clear sign that someone is out of control. Ones work very hard to stay in control of their emotions, surroundings, and fate. Anger threatens that control, so Ones avoid it at all costs, hoping to appear put-together, good, and wise. But this constant repression eventually bubbles to the surface! It can look like resentment, irritation, or passive aggressiveness. The root of this discontent is found in a desire to make the world the way it *should* be paired with frustration when reality inevitably fails to measure up.

THE SOLUTION: Picture yourself as a child. What brought you joy? At some point in your life, that playful energy was tamped down by a sense of duty and responsibility. But that childlike, innocent part of you is very important for your growth. Let yourself have fun and play!

- Find creative ways to express yourself.
- Don't run from your anger—it's there for a reason. Allow yourself to feel it, express it, and let it go.

TWO

PRIDE—Ignoring your own needs and charging forward; believing that you alone can fix everyone else's problems

Type Two's core weakness always surprises people. "What? But Twos are the most selfless people I know! How could that be true?" But pride comes in many forms, and for Twos, it looks like focusing all their attention and energy on meeting the needs of others while pretending that they have no needs of their own. This is rooted in a belief that others are way needier than they are. And they, being merciful and sacrificial martyrs, are the only ones who know how to solve the problem. Their motto becomes "I know what's best for everyone else . . . but *I'm* totally fine. Let's ignore what I need, want, think, and feel!"

THE SOLUTION: Self-care is so important for you, but I'm not only talking about bubble baths and face masks (although those *can* be fun). Your self-care needs to focus on setting and maintaining boundaries as well as doing intentional actions such as positive self-talk and nature walks.

- Say no to activities and people who drain you.
- Flight attendants will tell you to put on your own oxygen mask first before helping others. How can you help anyone else if you are running out of air? If you take care of yourself, you are better equipped to help the people around you.

THREE

DECEIT—Deceiving yourself into believing your intrinsic worth is based on your accomplishments

Threes fall into the trap of living for the way they look to others. More than anything, they want to feel admired and worthy of love. They try to achieve this by transforming their image into what they think others want to see. Sometimes, Threes are referred to as the chameleon of the Enneagram because they have the remarkable ability to shapeshift their personality. That's where the deceit comes from: not being truthful about who they actually are. But more than anything, the deceit is internal. Threes push aside their real feelings and desires to serve their image. They can forget their authentic selves, choosing instead to focus on productivity and achievement.

THE SOLUTION: Real, intentional rest. This doesn't mean watching TV for a few hours or scrolling online. This is an intentional time of rest every single week.

- What did you love doing as a child? Invest in those passions again.
- Try something new! Let yourself be bad at something and do it simply for the joy of it.

FOUR

ENVY— Feeling that you're missing a foundational and special quality that others seem to possess

When they are struggling with their core weakness, Fours come down with a bad case of comparison syndrome. But don't get this confused with jealousy! Envy is more about wanting a characteristic that other people possess. For example, it's not looking at Emily's beautiful house and thinking, "I want her house." It's looking at Emily's Craftsman home and her loving family and the way she seems to smile like there are no worries in the world and thinking, "I want whatever it is that she has that makes such a charmed life." At the end of the day, this thinking is rooted in the belief that they fundamentally lack something that everyone else seems to have. This can lead to feelings of inferiority and discontent.

THE SOLUTION: Lean into your growth arrow of Type One. What structures and routines can you build into your daily life to make sure you're still moving toward your goals? This can be difficult to do solo. May I suggest teaming up with a friend who can keep you accountable?

- Take a *big* break from social media. Seriously. Nothing about it is going to help you grow.
- Fours are *so* good at experiencing the beauty in the world. Don't let envy take that away from you. Look for beauty all around you. Revel in it. Make art about it.

FIVE

AVARICE—Hoarding inner resources (energy, personal information, and emotions) because you feel like too much interaction with others will lead to disastrous depletion of self

I had never heard the word *avarice* in normal conversation until I entered the Enneagram community. The formal definition is "extreme greed for wealth or material gain." But what really helped me grasp it was thinking about it like a dragon hoarding treasure. He knows that his stash is valuable and many people are willing to kill him to get it. So he protects it fiercely! Fives are like that dragon, but instead of rubies and gold coins, they are guarding their internal resources. They view the world as an intrusive place that takes and takes and takes. It's simply not safe for them to leave their energy, peace, and mind unprotected. Because of this, Fives don't look to friends or family when they have needs or problems. They turn to *knowledge* to give them that comfort. But this can become dangerous when they withdraw from people and opportunities, clutching their resources and minimizing their needs.

THE SOLUTION: It's okay to manage your energy reserve, just don't let fear hold you back from experiences.

- It's easy to fall back into the habit of constantly guarding your resources. But the truth is, the more you put yourself out there, the easier it gets. You have more energy and resources than you think you do.
- Your needs are not a burden, especially to the people who love you.

SIX

ANXIETY—Worrying about the past, present, and future; constantly anticipating worst-case scenarios

Inside every Six is a nagging voice constantly asking, "What if *this* happens? What if *that* happens?" They worry about the past, present, and future, anticipating worst-case scenarios around every corner. As you can imagine, it's hard to grow if you're constantly in a nail-biting state of worry. Ultimately, this is a trust issue. Struggling Sixes either don't trust themselves and look for reassurance in others *or* they don't trust others, so they look for reassurance by building up defenses. But growth is impossible if you are living in a constant state of fear.

THE SOLUTION: Do anything that helps bring you into the grounded present. This could be meditation, yoga, nature walks, or digital breaks.

- Breathe. Right now. Take a big ol' deep breath, in through the nose and out through the mouth. Notice how it makes you feel.

SEVEN

GLUTTONY—Constantly seeking to be fulfilled by the next experience or stimulation

Sevens feel an insatiable hunger inside of them. They want to experience all that life has to offer, so they throw themselves into new opportunities with wild abandon. On the outside, Sevens seem fearless. But the truth is, they are terrified of facing the reality of what's happening on the inside. They jump from experience to experience with the hope that the *next* thing will finally be the one that makes them happy. Only when Sevens learn to embrace their internal anxieties, sadness, and boredom can they truly grow.

THE SOLUTION: Focus on *one* thing. I know that sounds like deprivation, but think of it like a choice. You get to intentionally decide what one thing you are working toward.

- Let go of the things that are stressing you out, the ones you feel like you *have* to do but that don't necessarily contribute to your one main goal.
- Lean into those scary emotions, even when it feels uncomfortable.

EIGHT

EXCESS—Constantly desiring intensity, control, and power; steamrolling others to get what you want

Eights approach life with passion. This is one of their superpowers! They're *so* good at going after what they want and doing it with gusto! But this can lead Eights to live by the motto: "May the bridges I burn light the way." (Which, while many Eights find this hilarious, isn't the best strategy for becoming your healthiest self.) They become so self-focused that they steamroll other people, and even though they're not aware of it, they're also steamrolling themselves by cutting themselves off from a *huge* growth factor: vulnerability.

THE SOLUTION: Open up to others. I know it's scary, but vulnerability is the key to your personal growth.

- Take a step back from leadership. Instead, use your skills to mentor other people. Mentorship is an incredible gift you can give other people, and Eights are particularly good at it.

NINE

COMPLACENCY—Falling asleep to your inner passions and desires to keep the peace; refusing to acknowledge your anger

While Nines may love a blissful nap, they can actually be some of the hardest workers on the Enneagram! But when they are struggling with complacency, it's as if they're taking one long life nap. This happens when Nines strive to keep the peace by any means necessary. They'll suppress personal feelings and desires so as not to add one more voice to the fray. But eventually, all that chill "go along to get along" attitude makes things *really* uncomfortable because Nines feel like a shell of themselves, which makes anger and resentment bubble up from inside.

THE SOLUTION: Wake up to yourself! What do *you* want? Think deeply about who you want to be and the steps you need to take to get there.

- Build accountability. Tell others what you want in life and ask them to hold you to it.
- This is the most important step for Nines: Don't wait for the green light. Make a decision, take action, look at the result, and learn from it.

On a scale of 1–10, how much are you struggling with your core weakness right now?

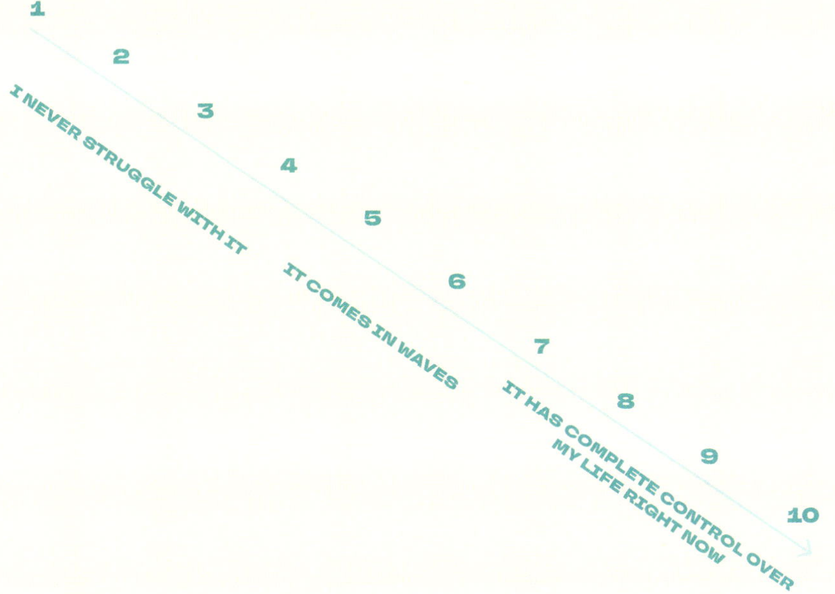

Share a time when this weakness harmed a personal or professional relationship.

Was there ever a time when someone called out your weakness or the negative traits associated with it? How did that make you feel?

Can you remember a time when you first felt this weakness take root? Think back to your childhood.

What fears do you have about facing this weakness?

Imagine your life without this weakness.
How different would it be?

What are things you can do to make that life a reality?

Setting Goals

THE GOAL-GETTERS: ONE, THREE, AND EIGHT

Ones, Threes, and Eights usually go after their goals with great pizzazz! But the problem with their enthusiasm is they can work themselves *so* hard that they're left burned out and resentful. Research shows us that the best way to get things done is to transform the daily grind into a source of daily joy. If these go-getter types can find ways to infuse breaks and play into their routine, they will unlock their hidden potential.

THE VOICE-CHALLENGED: TWO AND NINE

Some types don't even know what their goals are. Yep, Type Two and Type Nine, I'm looking at you! But their reasons are different.

Twos think, *"If I help everyone else achieve their goals, everyone will love and appreciate me!"* Nines think, *"If I say what I want, it might disrupt my comfort zone or cause conflict. I would rather stay peaceful and safe."*

I want you both to remember: Your needs matter! Plus, the people who truly want the best for you won't want you to bury your dreams. They want to help you achieve them!

THE DREAMERS: FOUR AND SEVEN

Fours and Sevens are typically brimming with ideas about how to make their lives better, but they struggle with follow-through. For Sevens, it's usually because they commit to *too* much, which totally sucks out the joy! Try picking just one or two top-priority goals and bringing them across the finish line.

Fours, on the other hand, experience a drop in motivation once the initial burst of passion has faded. Set yourself up for success by starting small and adding on gradually, like a runner training for a marathon. Nobody runs twenty-six miles cold turkey.

THE PREPPERS: FIVE AND SIX

I've got a quote for ya: "Good planning without good working is nothing." (Thanks, President Eisenhower!) See, Type Fives fear being incompetent. But they can spend *so* much time prepping for their goal that they never feel ready to actually . . . ya know, *do it*.

Meanwhile, Sixes can make ALL the lists in the world, but if they're not taking care of themselves, they're going to get overwhelmed. My advice? Ask for help. There's a reason accountability partners exist. Ask a trusted friend to keep you on track and encourage you when the going gets tough.

TAKE ACTION

TYPE ONE Pick an activity once a week that's not something you "should do," just what you *want* to do.

TYPE TWO For a couple of days a week, do an activity that brings you *joy*. Do it first thing in the morning so it always gets done!

TYPE THREE Take ten minutes weekly to write down what you're thankful for. But here's the challenge: Your gratitude list must be unrelated to your accomplishments and productivity.

TYPE FOUR After you eat breakfast, go on a fifteen-minute walk to start your day moving!

TYPE FIVE Track your progress. Bullet journaling is an excellent way to visually see how much you've accomplished and get a view of the big picture.

TYPE SIX Write. It. Down. Get it out of your brain and free up that space. Small progress is better than no progress!

TYPE SEVEN Spend one night a week by yourself working on a project or activity that matters to you.

TYPE EIGHT Incorporate stretch breaks throughout the workday. This gives your brain a breather and can help you reframe your thoughts to remember the *why* of your goals.

TYPE NINE Ask a friend for coffee to talk about what you're passionate about and help you plan actionable steps!

1-EXERCISE: MAP YOUR FULFILLMENT

Shade in each piece of the pie to indicate how happy you feel in that area of life. For example, if you're 100 percent content in that area of your life, fill up the entire section! If there's room to grow, fill it up 25 percent. I highly recommend using colored pens or pencils—it's more fun and helps distinguish each section from the others.

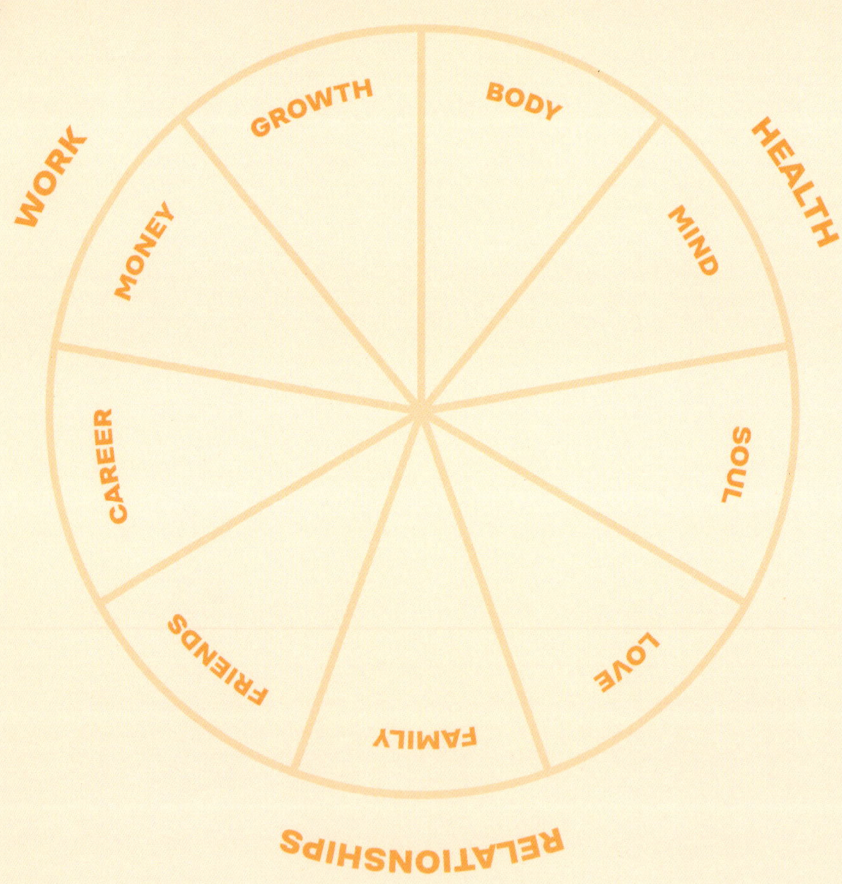

What are your three lowest categories?

Why do you think you scored lowest in these categories?

Do you see any correlations between your three lowest categories and your type's core weakness? For example, as an Enneagram Three with the core weakness of deceit, I scored lowest in mind, body, and soul. These are areas of my life that I neglect while I'm struggling to keep up the appearance of being successful and productive. When I am paying attention to those areas, it's a healthy sign that I am growing as a person.

2-YOUR NEXT SIX MONTHS

Using the results from your fulfillment map, let's create an action plan for the next six months.

Fill in the three columns heads with your three lowest categories. Now brainstorm! What can you do to bring up your fulfillment levels in these categories during the next six months?

EXERCISE

3-ACTION PLAN

Pick one idea from your brainstorming list to focus on each month. Get specific! Write the exact days and times that you will be completing this action. If you're a calendar person, get it on your Google calendar, your paper planner, etc.

Month 1: My one focus is ____________________

The ideal result looks like . . .	To get started, I will . . .	I will make this a habit in my life by . . .

Month 2: My one focus is ____________________

The ideal result looks like . . .	To get started, I will . . .	I will make this a habit in my life by . . .

Month 3: My one focus is ____________________

The ideal result looks like . . .	To get started, I will . . .	I will make this a habit in my life by . . .

Month 4: My one focus is ____________________

The ideal result looks like . . .	To get started, I will . . .	I will make this a habit in my life by . . .

Month 5: My one focus is ____________________

The ideal result looks like . . .	To get started, I will . . .	I will make this a habit in my life by . . .

Month 6: My one focus is ____________________

The ideal result looks like . . .	To get started, I will . . .	I will make this a habit in my life by . . .

ALL ABOUT WINGS

On the Enneagram symbol, there are numbers to the left and right of your main type. For example, if your main type is a Three, then your neighbor numbers are Two and Four. These neighbor numbers are called your wings.

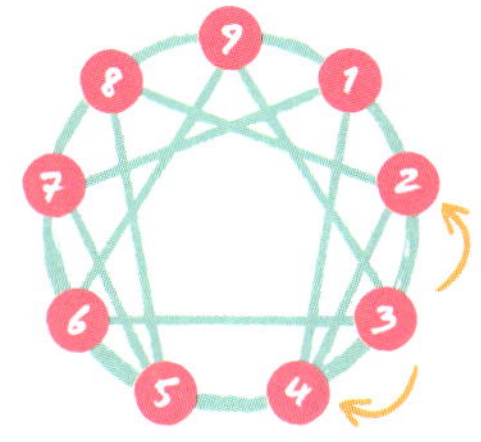

What Do Wings Do?

Think of wings as flavoring for your personality. They add spice to your main Enneagram type and give you a more well-rounded picture of your full self!

How Do I Find My Dominant Wing?

You'll find that most people lean more heavily on one wing than the other, and this leaning makes their main Enneagram type look different. People will distinguish their dominant wing by writing a small "w" next to their main type with the wing number following. For example, a Three who finds themselves using traits from their Two wing more often because they have a more service-based, relational job will write their type like this:

A Note About the Origins of the Wing Names:

The names for each wing combination are sourced from The Enneagram Institute, founded in 1997 by the late Don Richard Riso and Russ Hudson.

Can I Display Both My Wings?

We all have access to the strengths and weaknesses of both our wings. For example, when faced with a social event around their crush, a Type Three could lean on their Two wing to stand out, charm, and attract their crush. When faced with a business problem, a Type Three could lean on their Four wing to hunker down and figure out a creative solution. However, you probably have one wing that you lean on more often than the other (a.k.a. your dominant wing).

Your dominant wing influences how your main Enneagram type expresses itself—sometimes complementing it, other times creating tension by introducing conflicting traits.

Take a Type Eight, for instance. They can have a dominant wing of either Seven or Nine. A dominant Seven wing complements the Eight's natural intensity, adding high energy and a drive for personal fulfillment. On the other hand, a dominant Nine wing introduces contrasting qualities, as Nines tend to approach situations more calmly and passively than Eights. As a result, Eights with a Nine wing may experience inner conflict, while those with a Seven wing tend to feel more naturally aligned, as their instincts are fully in sync.

This pairing blends well together

This pairing clashes with each other

TYPE ONE WINGS

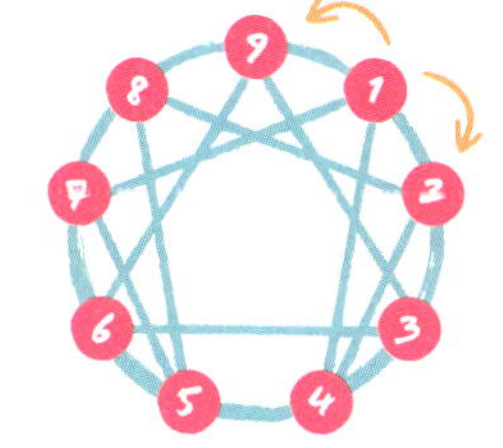

1w2 The Advocate

They are **socially-aware activists** who work to **create a better world** for the people around them. They tend to be more **helpful and empathetic** and are very **action-oriented**. This type also longs to control everything and **struggles with letting go**.

1w9 The Idealist

They are **practical perfectionists** who tend to be more **introverted**. They excel at **objective thinking** and can become quite detached and self-neglectful when things in their life get stressful. The Nine brings out a more **trusting**, **relaxed nature in the One**, making them able to hold a **more diplomatic stance toward others with different viewpoints**.

TYPE TWO WINGS

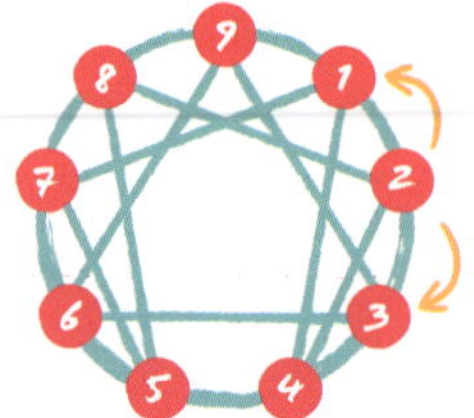

2w1 The Servant

They are **empathetic** individuals who **long to make others happy**. They tend to be generous, **giving to anyone who has a need**, not just people they like. This type is **honest with themselves** and directs their energy toward **fixing the things they believe should improve**. They struggle with **burnout** because they can overwork themselves in an effort to **help the underdog**.

2w3 The Host

They are **outgoing and productive organizers** who excel at bringing people together. They tend to be **charming** and **ambitious** with a **competitive** spirit. This wing pairing brings the risk of **workaholism**, influenced by Three's emphasis on **work and success**. They love it when other **people like them,** and they will **move mountains both socially and professionally** to make that happen.

TYPE THREE WINGS

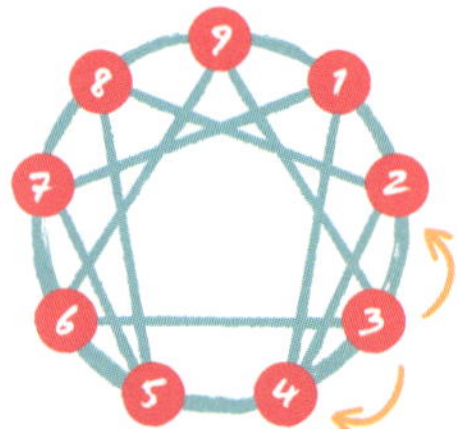

3w2 The Star

They are **socially-savvy** people who are extremely **interpersonal** and **charismatic**. They tend to enjoy being the center of attention and **thrive when they are popular**. These Threes struggle with **being true to themselves** because they are always outwardly focused on others' expectations.

3w4 The Professional

They are **driven** and **organized** individuals who always have **new ideas and projects in the works**. They tend to be more **introverted** and find **quiet satisfaction** in efficiency and personal success. Their Four wing also means they lean more toward the **creative** and **imaginative** but can withdraw from others, feeling **moody** and **detached**.

TYPE FOUR WINGS

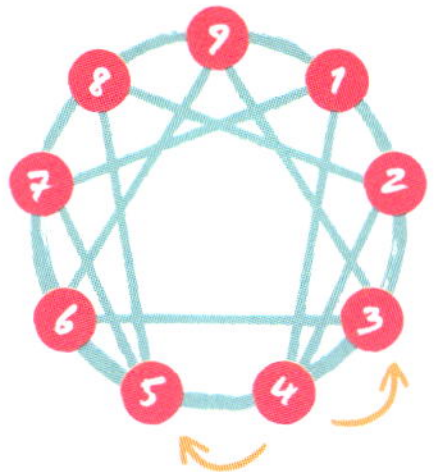

4w3 The Aristocrat

They are **charismatic artists** who value **nature** and **beauty**. They tend to be more **extroverted**, **ambitious**, and **competitive** with a **large emotional range**. A challenge for the 4w3 is that they may try to escape their inner turmoil by **performing and valuing form without substance** instead of engaging in beneficial inner work.

4w5 The Bohemian

They are **intense creators** who use self-expression to **explore the world** and what it means to be human. They tend to be more **introverted** and **intellectual** with a high capacity for **thoughtful observation**. This type is prone to **withdrawing from others** when depressed. The Four and Five together are an **odd combination** because they are able to **balance artistic intuition with reason and logic**.

TYPE FIVE WINGS

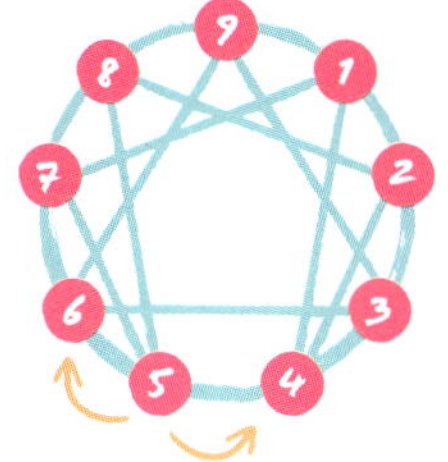

5w4 The Iconoclast

They are **lone rangers** who value being self-taught. They tend to be more **creative and humanistic**, and can take an intense interest in one subject. Like the 4w5, they have the peculiar gift of being able to **balance the right and left brain**. This type can struggle with feeling **misunderstood** and may become **depressed and self-absorbed**.

5w6 The Problem Solver

They are **detached researchers** who are energized by **discovering new things**. They tend to be more **outgoing** and **loyal**. Their Six wing makes it easier for them to connect deeply with other people. They struggle with **skepticism and self-isolation** when they feel distrustful of others.

TYPE SIX WINGS

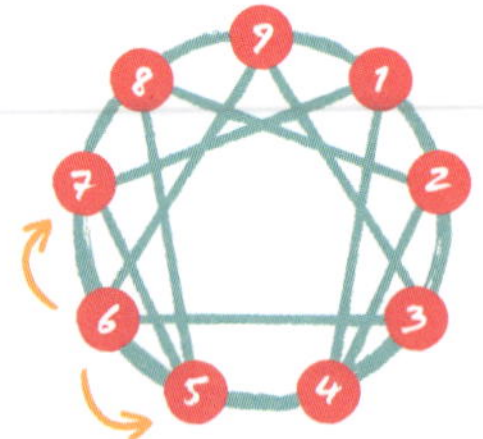

6w5 The Defender

They are **resourceful team players** who value **security** and **knowledge**. They tend to be more **introverted** and **cautious** with an ability to make **reasonable decisions and sound judgments**. They can **back away from confrontation** instead of dealing with issues head-on.

6w7 The Buddy

They are **optimistic explorers** who embrace **fun**. The 6w7 is a strange dichotomy because while they are **spontaneous and playful**, they also have a **strong need for safety and security**. They have a Six's **fear of pain** combined with a Seven's **avoidance of pain**, which can create **withdrawal from life** by encouraging them to dive into **trivial distractions**.

TYPE SEVEN WINGS

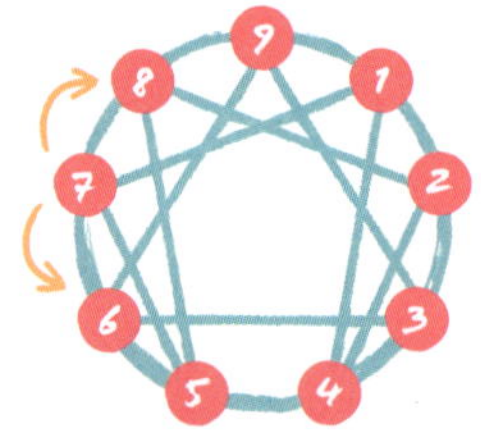

7w6 The Entertainer

They are a **happy-go-lucky fun chaser**! They always want **new experiences** and projects to fill their days. They tend to be **loyal**, **playful**, **and very interpersonal**. A main challenge of this wing combo is that they may **exaggerate underlying fears** and struggle with **anxiety and self-doubt**.

7w8 The Realist

They are **innovative entrepreneurs** and **leaders** who love **exploring** and **creating**. They tend to be **free-spirited and passionate**. A challenge with this pairing is that their assertiveness can become **aggressive**, and they can act **superior** to others.

TYPE EIGHT WINGS

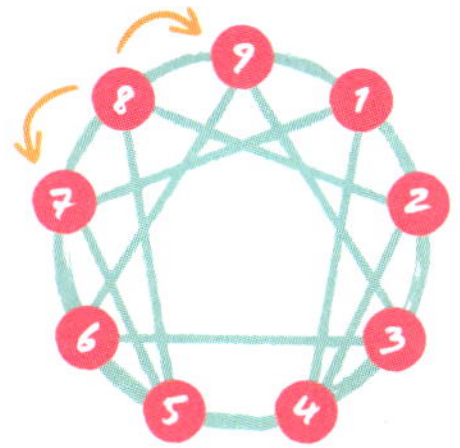

8w7 The Maverick

They are **confident self-starters** who use their **enterprising**, **fearless** spirits to conquer the world. They tend to be more **extroverted** and **energetic**, with a heavy focus on finding their own power. This type struggles with being **reflective on the consequences of their actions**.

8w9 The Bear

They are **quietly strong leaders** who strive to preserve **harmony** in a **gentle way**. They keep others' best interests in mind and tend to be **more people-oriented than 8w7s**. This wing combo struggles with **withdrawing in stressful times** and then **judging themselves for that behavior**.

TYPE NINE WINGS

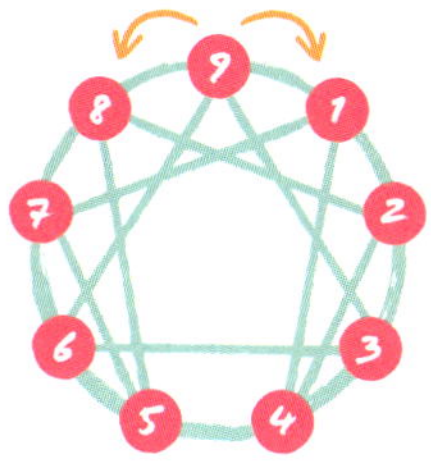

9w1 The Dreamer

They are **idealistic romantics** who are able to balance their **meditative nature** with **pragmatic perspectives**. They tend to be **introverted** and **compliant**, and they value being **connected to others in their community**. A challenge for this pairing is that they may be even **less expressive of their needs** because **they don't want to alienate others**.

9w8 The Comfort-Seeker

They are **independent individuals** with a calm mission to **discover the world**. They tend to be **outgoing**, **assertive**, **and active** with the ability to balance **diplomacy** and **individuality**. They struggle with the **pursuit of pleasure** rather than focusing on the **genuine needs of their real self**.

In this section, we covered core weaknesses, goal setting, and wings. What tools from this section do you want to implement into your daily life?

In the Map Your Fulfillment exercise on page 152, did your three lowest categories surprise you? Why or why not?

When you look at the different focuses you wrote down in your action plan, which one excites you the most? Why do you think that is the case?

Pay attention to your personality traits as you navigate your daily life. Which wing do you find yourself relying on more? This is your dominant wing.

How have you seen your dominant wing influence your main type? Give an example.

How does it impact your relationships, work, hobbies, and daily life?

How does your secondary wing influence your main type?

What would it look like for your wings to be equally balanced?

FOUR
LOVE
BET

OTHERS
TER

“The trick to healthy relationships is to be healthy. It doesn’t have anything to do with your number.”

—SUZANNE STABILE,
THE ENNEAGRAM GODMOTHER

BETTER TOGETHER

When my husband, Jon, and I first started dating, we met up for an after-work date at our favorite dumpling spot. As soon as we sat down, I noticed something was off—his usual easygoing smile and jokey manner were missing. He explained that a work conflict was weighing on him. Instinctively, I jumped into problem-solving mode, laying out a game plan, and telling him exactly what he should do the next day. But as I strategized, I could feel him pulling away.

What I didn't realize then—but understand now—is that I was offering the kind of support I would want as a Type Three: a quick, actionable solution to push through discomfort. But Jon, a Type Four, needed something different. He didn't need a strategy; he needed presence. He needed me to sit with him, listen, and empathize rather than try to fix things. Now, after years of marriage and a baby, we still use the knowledge of our types to love one another better.

I truly believe that so many misunderstandings and conflicts could be easily resolved if we used this tool more often, and not just in romantic relationships. The Enneagram has the power to deepen connections between family, friends, and coworkers. I hope you can use the wisdom in the following section to do just that.

A Friendly Reminder

One of the biggest gifts of the Enneagram is how it helps us understand and love others better. But I need to warn you about a common trap that can totally derail someone's journey: typing other people without their input. Why? It gives more weight to your projections of another person's type than to their internal experience. Please don't be ashamed if you've done this . . . Everyone goes through this phase when they first learn about the Enneagram; I certainly did! I made my poor dad take an Enneagram test three separate times because I didn't believe he was the type he was getting. It's hard not to want your loved ones to experience the same life-changing transformation that you did!

But the issue is that it prevents people from experiencing the Enneagram for themselves. Plus, even if someone displays stereotypical behavior of a number, you can't definitively know the core motivation *behind* that behavior.

That doesn't mean you can't use your knowledge of the Enneagram to guide your interactions with others, even if they haven't discovered their type yet. It is totally okay to notice that your boss is showing a lot of signs of being a Type One or that the person you're dating seems to have a Type Seven's core fear. Use the tools in this section to help you observe and communicate with them better. Just don't assume you know them better than they know themselves. They've got to do this journey on their own!

HOW TO LOVE A TYPE ONE

Type Ones in My Life:

VALUE THEIR TIME: On a surface level, this means don't be late. But on a deeper level, if you're not enjoying the relationship, tell them how you're feeling. Otherwise you're just wasting their time . . . and yours!

CREATE A PEACEFUL ENVIRONMENT: Ones desire a beautiful environment to promote peace in their inner and outer lives. So stay organized and keep your shared space decluttered and clean.

BE THE SHOULDER ANGEL: When they are struggling, Ones have an inner critic that judges their every move. When you sense that little shoulder devil is being unreasonably harsh, counter the criticism like a shoulder angel. Be a voice of grace, empathy, and understanding.

DO YOUR FAIR SHARE: Make sure to take on your share of responsibilities so the One doesn't end up doing all the work. Get that shared Google Calendar up and running. *Actually* follow the chore chart. Launch a discussion about the ethics of the division of labor in modern households.

WELCOME THEIR INNER CHILD: When Ones grow, they release the need to be perfect. This looks like trying something new or searching for joy in their daily life. So encourage your One here! Listen to their worries and concerns to help them lighten up. Plan a fun activity to do together that speaks to their inner child.

Encouraging Things to Say to a One:

"How can I make your job easier?"

"You are a good person."

"What is something fun that you want to do today?"

CONFLICT SUPERPOWER: Discuss facts over feelings.

What is a trait you admire about Ones?

Was there an instance where you did or said the wrong thing for a Type One?

List ways you can better love the Ones in your life. A great starting point is to reach out directly and ask Ones about the best way to love them.

HOW TO LOVE A TYPE TWO

Type Twos in My Life:

GIVE THEM HUGS: Most Enneagram Twos have physical affection as one of their love languages. If affection is a part of your relationship, give them a back massage! Hold their hand during a movie! Let them know in small, tangible ways that you care about them.

PLAN A COFFEE DATE: You will often need to straight up ask a Two what they need. So ask them out for a cup of coffee for just that purpose. Make it clear that meeting their needs is a joy for you (the same way it feels to them when they help someone).

TAKE A CHILL PILL: Because of their extreme empathy, not only do they feel their feelings, but they also feel *your* feelings. So if tensions are high and you're both upset, wait until emotions have cooled off to talk about it.

GO TO THAT *LORD OF THE RINGS* CONVENTION: The interests of those around them can often overshadow their own interests. So show Twos love by taking interest in their favorite hobby. If it's musical theater, learn the lyrics to "Alexander Hamilton"! If it's drinking wine, take them to a winery! If it's going to *Lord of the Rings* conventions, get yourself a hobbit cloak.

AFFIRM THEIR SOUL MESSAGE: Twos struggle with believing that they are enough just the way they are. How can you show your love for the Twos in your life while also emphasizing that this love isn't dependent on how much they are helping you? Does that look like affirming them when they delegate or practice self-care? Or going out of your way to send them encouragement texts?

Encouraging Things to Say to a Two:

CONFLICT SUPERPOWER: Use the sandwich method—first, say an affirmation, then say the issue at hand, followed by more affirmation.

What is a trait you admire about Twos?

Was there an instance where you did or said the wrong thing for a Type Two?

List ways you can better love the Twos in your life. A great starting point is to reach out directly and ask Twos about the best way to love them.

HOW TO LOVE A TYPE THREE

Type Threes in My Life:

SAY WORDS OF AFFIRMATION: There is nothing better than my husband telling me that he's proud of me and naming specific reasons why. But don't just shower Threes with vague platitudes. Give them intentional, specific reasons behind the affirmation.

SEPARATE THEIR ACCOMPLISHMENTS FROM LOVE: Somewhere along the way, Threes received the message that they are only worthy of love based on their achievements. Refute that by telling them that you value them simply for being who they are and not for the things they check off their to do list. This speaks to the longings of their heart.

KEEP AN EYE OUT: When Enneagram Threes are struggling, they can be impatient and easily frustrated. They have difficulty processing and discussing what's going on emotionally. So try to recognize when a Three may be exhibiting symptoms of detachment and fogginess. If they desire personal growth, I don't think they will mind a gentle directional reminder that they need to check in with what's going on inside.

INVEST IN REST: If you see that a Three may be inching toward burnout, invite them to spend an intentional day away from work. Leave the phone and computer at home. Go to the beach with a book that has nothing to do with their job. Go for a hike, but don't talk about goals or plans for the future.

TIDY UP: Threes operate at their best when their home is clean and organized. So a good way to show love to a Three in the household is to always do your dishes after you cook, put your laundry away after you wash it, and regularly scrub down the shower. If resources allow, hire someone to come and clean your house once a month!

Encouraging Things to Say to a Three:

"I'm proud of you."

"You are a human being; not a human doing."

"I love you simply for who you are."

CONFLICT SUPERPOWER: Instead of dwelling on failures, keep the conversation focused on actionable solutions.

What is a trait you admire about Threes?

Was there an instance where you did or said the wrong thing for a Type Three?

List ways you can better love the Threes in your life. A great starting point is to reach out directly and ask Threes about the best way to love them.

HOW TO LOVE A TYPE FOUR

Type Fours in My Life:

FEEL THE FEELINGS: It's tough for other Enneagram numbers to discuss feelings the way Fours do. When my (Type Four) husband Jon and I first started dating, he was always asking, "How are you feeling?" But he was never satisfied with my typical "I'm fine" response. Fours aren't afraid to get comfortable with the uncomfortable. So be vulnerable with how you *really* feel. Fours will appreciate the authenticity, and it will help your relationship flourish.

HONOR THE SILENCE: Don't try to fill the silence with noise or questions. Quiet moments can be a sweet space to share.

GIVE THEM AUTHENTIC COMPLIMENTS: All of their lives, Fours have felt that they are inherently lacking. To help with that internal messaging, tell them what makes them special. One little warning though: sometimes Fours have a hard time receiving compliments. This isn't something that you can change, but it's helpful to be aware of this trait.

DON'T CHEER THEM UP: Fours enjoy the sweetness of life while not ignoring the bitterness that we all face being alive on this planet. Fours reject the rose-colored glasses that some Enneagram types wear as a wardrobe staple. They reflect deeply on tragedies. They cry at concerts, church, and work. But you don't need to cheer them up if they are sitting with something difficult. It's okay to let them feel.

REACH FOR YOUR DREAMS: Fours can get overwhelmed with the details of how to bring their big ideas into reality. If you have the gift of planning, help them create structure to make it happen.

Encouraging Things to Say to a Four:

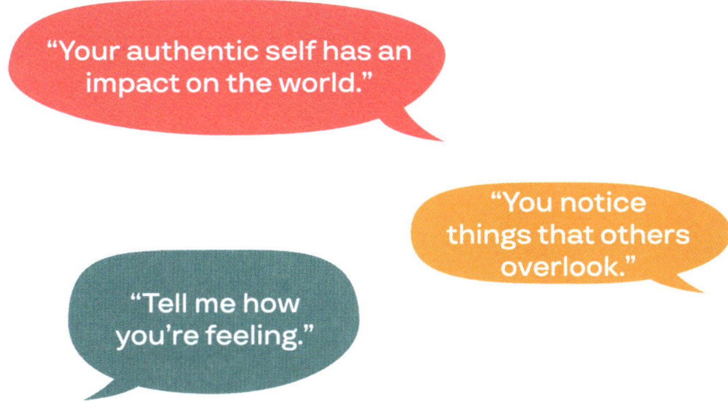

CONFLICT SUPERPOWER: Be as authentic as possible, even if the outcome is messy.

What is a trait you admire about Fours?

Was there an instance where you did or said the wrong thing for a Type Four?

List ways you can better love the Fours in your life. A great starting point is to reach out directly and ask Fours about the best way to love them.

HOW TO LOVE A TYPE FIVE

Type Fives in My Life:

TO KNOW THEIR HEART, START WITH THEIR HEAD: If you see a Five in a tough situation, don't ask them how they feel or try to empathize with whatever feelings you think they might be having. It's not that Fives don't have feelings; they just prefer to deal with them privately. Instead, ask questions that can help them understand their situation from an outside perspective.

TAKE THEIR FEAR SERIOUSLY: Want to know what keeps Fives up at night? Incompetence. That's why they spend so much time and energy collecting knowledge and making sure they are self-sufficient! So be as respectful and aware as possible when you are discussing a Five's feelings of inadequacy.

TELL ME MORE: Fives often take an intense interest in certain subjects. A wonderful way to connect with your Five is to sit down and ask them about the topics they care about. (Just ask Ron Swanson how to build a chair from local walnut tree or why he calls his favorite whiskey the "nectar of the gods." You might be there for a while.)

LEAVE 'EM ALONE: Fives have a limited amount of energy. That's why time alone is so important! It may be difficult to not take this personally, but keep in mind that they don't want to be alone because they don't like *you*. Rather, they need time alone so they can be the best version of themselves *for* you.

MAKE IT THE SAME: Fives thrive on predictability! When managers ask how best to care for Fives, that's what I tell them. Don't spring unexpected stuff on them, like a last-minute meeting that definitely should've been an email.

Encouraging Things to Say to a Five:

CONFLICT SUPERPOWER: Give them time to process their thoughts and feelings alone.

What is a trait you admire about Fives?

Was there an instance where you did or said the wrong thing for a Type Five?

List ways you can better love the Fives in your life. A great starting point is to reach out directly and ask Fives about the best way to love them.

HOW TO LOVE A TYPE SIX

Type Sixes in My Life:

LOL: Most Sixes have an incredible sense of humor. When you're constantly preparing for the worst-case scenario, you've got to be able to laugh a little, right? But when they're anxious, that joyful nature disappears behind a million worries. I'm not telling you to brush off their anxiety; however, don't be afraid to be silly. Tell a joke! Do a weird character you've invented! If you can find a way to get them laughing, it's a huge stress reliever.

LET YOUR ACTIONS SPEAK: Do what you say you're going to do. Show up when you need to show up. Try your best to make your actions and words a sure thing. This will bring a level of comfort and relief to a Six and allow them to thrive within any relationship.

HONOR THEIR ABILITY TO BE DEVIL'S ADVOCATE: We need risk-averse thinkers in our lives. Otherwise, we would find ourselves vastly unprepared for difficult situations!

REASSURE THEM: Remind them that it's okay to be anxious; it's literally your body's way of keeping you safe! But it doesn't always have to be overpowering. As we grow older and wiser, we (hopefully) find tools to help us manage those feelings. Help them along this journey by letting them know they're not alone.

BE THEIR BIGGEST FAN: One of the marriage vows Jon and I made was to be each other's biggest fan, both publicly and privately. If you want to build a healthy relationship with a Six, do just that! Sixes are notoriously loyal people. They support you, but they really need someone to support them.

Encouraging Things to Say to a Six:

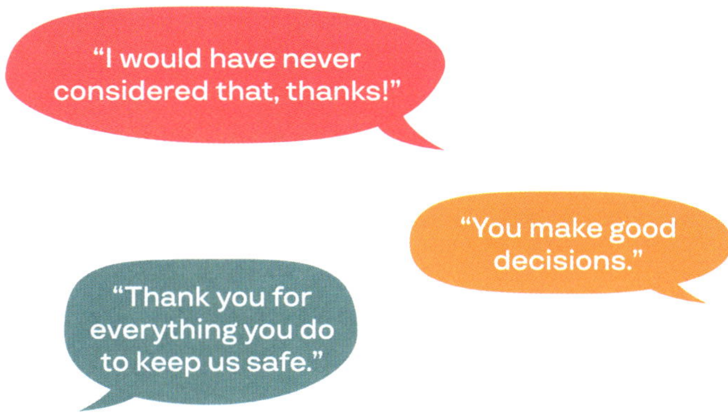

CONFLICT SUPERPOWER: Don't brush off their fears. Listen to them. Make them feel valued and safe.

What is a trait you admire about Sixes?

Was there an instance where you did or said the wrong thing for a Type Six?

List ways you can better love the Sixes in your life. A great starting point is to reach out directly and ask Sixes about the best way to love them.

HOW TO LOVE A TYPE SEVEN

Type Sevens in My Life:

REFRAME THE REFRAME: Sevens avoid negative emotions at all costs, preferring to look on the bright side. But reframing can be frustrating in relationships. My advice, ironically, is to reframe how you see this tendency. It's not immaturity or an unwillingness to address problems. Rather, it's a form of self-protection. And they've been doing it since they were kids! Your Seven is just doing their best to survive in that moment.

SPEND QUALITY TIME: Sevens value one-on-one attention that says, "Hey! I value doing things with you!" So be intentional about spending quality time with them. When you are with your Seven, be with *them*, not your phone.

RECOGNIZE THE SIGNS OF BOREDOM: Sevens can jump from thing to thing to avoid boredom. But all that busyness is masking what's actually going on inside. When you notice this behavior, check in with them. Ask them what they're feeling, and give them space to share that.

JUST SAY NO (TO ROUTINE): Come to terms with the fact that Sevens need flexibility in life so they don't feel trapped and deprived. If you're a planner, this might be tough for you to handle, but know that you are actively caring for your Seven when you give them space to be spontaneous.

DO YOUR OWN THING: Though Sevens enjoy the company of their friends and family, they don't require constant companionship. Because the truth is, they've got their own thing going on: lots of interests and hobbies that might not align with you! So a great way to love on your Seven is to have your own interests and friend circles. This will make your relationship thrive.

Encouraging Things to Say to a Seven:

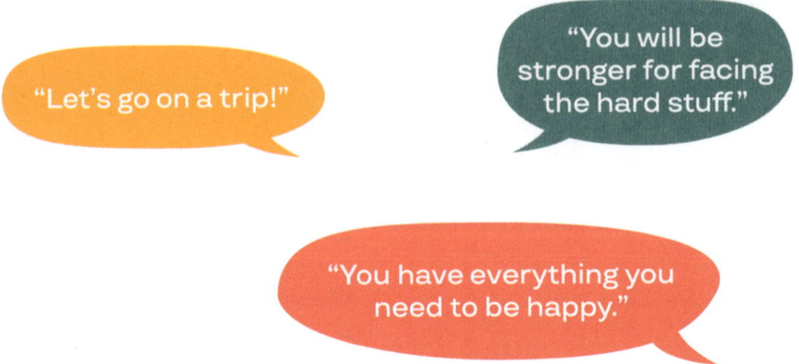

CONFLICT SUPERPOWER: Keep the conversation upbeat and positive. Remain open to their creative solutions.

What is a trait you admire about Sevens?

Was there an instance where you did or said the wrong thing for a Type Seven?

List ways you can better love the Sevens in your life. A great starting point is to reach out directly and ask Sevens about the best way to love them.

HOW TO LOVE A TYPE EIGHT

Type Eights in My Life:

LISTEN TO THEM: My mom is a Type Eight and often tells a story from her first year of marriage when my dad was still learning to listen. For their first Christmas, my dad spent their entire budget to buy her a Walkman. He assumed she would like it because it's the kind of gift he would like. But the problem was my mom didn't listen to music that much and had already stated that she wanted a new pair of shoes. Thirty-four years later, the Walkman still comes up in conversation occasionally. So listen to your Eight, folks.

PRACTICE WHAT YOU PREACH: Eights fear being betrayed. I know the word *betrayed* can seem dramatic, but little betrayals happen daily. If you say one thing and then do another, you're betraying your word. So do your best to make your word your bond.

BE THE STRONG ONE: Eights use their strength to plow a path for their friends, families, and partners. But if you've ever had to be the strong one, you know it can get exhausting. Sometimes, Eights need you to stand up for yourself *and* for them.

STOP BEATING AROUND THE BUSH: Eights value direct and honest communication. So just get straight to the point!

RELEASE THOSE ENDORPHINS: Eights have a lot of intensity, whether that be anger, passion, or just excess energy. That's why it's *so* important for Eights to move their bodies regularly. Encourage them to find movement that brings them joy. If that means being their hiking buddy, grab some almonds and lace up your boots.

Encouraging Things to Say to an Eight:

CONFLICT SUPERPOWER: Give them the benefit of the doubt. Just because they are blunt doesn't automatically mean they are attacking you.

What is a trait you admire about Eights?

Was there an instance where you did or said the wrong thing for a Type Eight?

List ways you can better love the Eights in your life. A great starting point is to reach out directly and ask Eights about the best way to love them.

HOW TO LOVE A TYPE NINE

Type Nines in My Life:

REMEMBER THE BIG AND SMALL THINGS: I asked a Nine friend of mine what he needs in a partner, and he said, "I want my partner to hear and remember things I say and share—both little details and big vulnerable things." This may seem like a "well, duh" kind of thing for some of you, but Nines have spent most of their lives being unwilling wallflowers. Make sure they feel like their voice is important.

ASK THEM QUESTIONS: Get to know your Nine by asking them questions and taking a genuine interest in the answers.

BANISH THE WORD "LAZY": This should be a no-brainer, but I'm putting it in writing just in case. If a Nine is low energy, it does not mean they're lazy. It may be they're overwhelmed by the energy needed to exist in the world. Nines are *very* empathetic, so they spend every day soaking up other people's needs and energies. How draining! Just keeping that in mind can give you a whole new level of understanding for the Nines in your life.

THROW A PARTY: Nines are truly at their best when they have the confidence to acknowledge their needs and voice their opinions. So when you notice a Nine being assertive, throw them a freaking party!

COZY UP: Soft rain on a window, long naps, a hot cup of tea, freshly washed sheets . . . What do these things have in common? They're cozy! Nines celebrate things that bring peace, warmth, and comfort. Find a way to elevate their cozy experience or just enjoy it with them!

Encouraging Things to Say to a Nine:

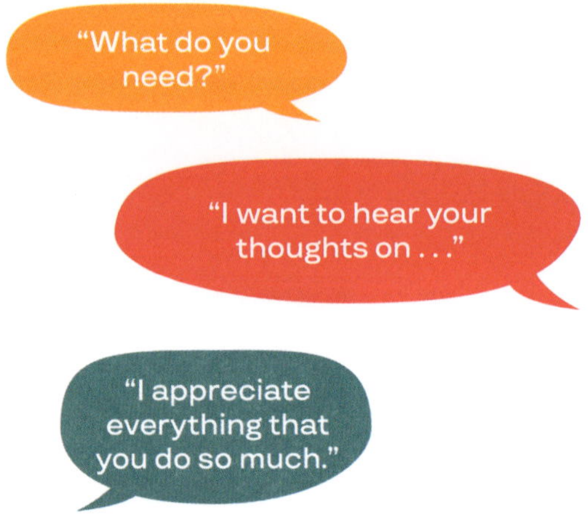

CONFLICT SUPERPOWER: Never interrupt or talk over a Nine. This just reaffirms their belief that their voice doesn't matter.

What is a trait you admire about Nines?

Was there an instance where you did or said the wrong thing for a Type Nine?

List ways you can better love the Nines in your life. A great starting point is to reach out directly and ask Nines about the best way to love them.

Write a letter to your future self so you can look back on this time in your life and reflect on how far you've come. Here are some prompts to help you get the ball rolling:

- What behavior or pattern do I want to change?
- How will my future self be different from who I am now?
- What actions am I going to take to get there?
- How does my future self act, feel, and look?
- What does my future self believe?

A Note from Me to You

Dear Reader,

I want you to give yourself a round of applause. Or pat yourself on the back. Or treat yourself to your favorite ice cream. Whatever feels like a celebration of your hard work. Because this journey isn't easy and, quite frankly, not everyone has the guts to do it. Go you!

I hope the tools you learned in this guide stick with you as you find your voice, say yes to that first date, or go to bed early just because your body needs it. I hope you move with confidence and wisdom as you manage your core weakness, maintain a boundary, or finally step into your purpose. But most of all, my hope is that you feel equipped to seek out the best version of you.

Thank you for trusting me to lead you. There are so many wonderful Enneagram teachers out there, and I'm honored you put your faith in me. Now, this may be end of our guide, but it doesn't have to be the end of our time together. If you want to keep learning, laughing, and growing with me, you can find more resources and encouragement here:

- Substack: talkenneagram.substack.com
- Instagram: @enneagramwithabbey
- TikTok: @abbey_howe
- YouTube: youtube.com/abbeyhowe
- Website: abbeyhowe.com

Happy discovering, friend!

Acknowledgments

This book is only possible because of the enthusiasm, support, and input of my online community. Thank you for following, engaging, and sending videos that resonate to your friends and family. Thank you for your thoughtful insights in DMs, emails, and comments. Our conversations around the Enneagram teach me so much more than any other resource could.

Thank you to Jon Frisch, my husband, my in-home lighting director, my personal inspirational speaker, my proofreader, and my Type Four test subject. Thank you for keeping me going when I thought I couldn't. I couldn't ask for a better teammate and friend. I love you, Noaf.

To our son who grew in my belly as I wrote this book: You are my life's light. Thank you for helping this Type Three mom separate her worth from her productivity.

To my parents, Penny and Alan, for your love, prayer, and cheerleading. And for watching that three-hour high school production of *King Lear* not once, but multiple times. I hope to live up to your example of patient and loving parenting.

To my editor, Jill Saginario, as well as Tony Ong, Peggy Gannon, and Rachel Sims for championing this idea and seeing it through to the finish line. You guys are awesome!

To Jordan Kay for bringing this book to life with your illustrations. You are incredibly talented, and I'm so lucky you came on board.

Thank you to Jen Worick for reaching out years ago and starting the process of this book. Your encouragement and support made this a worthwhile adventure.

To Amanda Orozco, my agent, for your guidance, wisdom, and giving the best book recommendations.

To Seriina, my Cafe de Leche writing buddy, for your company and friendship. To Shiloh and Dana for being my beta readers.

To Carissa and Jon, Becca, Dylan, Jillaine, Charlotte, David, Sarina, Stacey, and Sally for providing stories for the Enneagram IRL sections.

To all the Enneagram teachers who came before me, whose work and contributions changed my life: Beatrice Chestnut, Sarajane Case, Ian Morgan Cron, Suzanne Stabile, Richard Rohr, Russ Hudson, Uranio Paes, and Beth McCord.

And to Lemon for sitting at my feet while I write and being the absolute cutest.

Further Reading

The Road Back to You by Ian Morgan Cron and Suzanne Stabile
This was my first introduction to the Enneagram! I love it because it takes a story-based approach to the Enneagram while exploring the more spiritual aspects of this tool.

Burnout: The Secret to Unlocking the Stress Cycle by Drs. Amelia and Emily Nagoski
This isn't an Enneagram book, but the tools I've learned for understanding and preventing burnout are a perfect complement to Enneagram work—every type faces burnout in their own way!

Take Care of Your Type: An Enneagram Guide to Self-Care by Christina Wilcox
This delightful little book goes hand-in-hand with the quest to prevent burnout and handle stress. It provides creative and insightful tools for taking care of yourself based on your type.

The Complete Enneagram: 27 Paths to Greater Self-Knowledge by Beatrice Chestnut
Instinctual subtypes bring depth, context, and awareness to your Enneagram type. While I couldn't expand on them in this workbook, I encourage you to explore them further. A great place to start is with Beatrice Chestnut, PhD who was the first to put all twenty-seven subtypes into an accessible guide. Her expertise has been invaluable in shaping my own understanding of the Enneagram. If you're interested in diving deeper into her work, I highly recommend her book or her online school, CP Enneagram Academy, which she co-runs with Uranio Paes.

The Honest Enneagram: Know Your Type, Own Your Challenges, Embrace Your Growth by Sarajane Case
This is a great beginner's book that takes a gentle approach to self-awareness. I love the way the author represents each type in a caring, beautiful manner.

The Enneagram for Black Liberation by Chichi Agorom
If you're seeking healing in this insane world, look no further! Though everyone can (and should!) learn from this book, it speaks directly to Black readers to help them return to their truest selves in a system that seeks to dampen their self-worth and belonging.

ABOUT Abbey Howe

PHOTO © ASHLYN KUDRANSKY

Meet your new Enneagram BFF! Abbey Howe is a certified Enneagram coach known for her lighthearted, relatable approach to personality and self-discovery. With over ten million views across platforms like YouTube, Instagram, and TikTok, she creates engaging, educational content that makes the Enneagram accessible for everyone. Abbey works with teams around the world—from global companies to local community groups—helping people build self-awareness, empathy, and stronger relationships. Her mission? To help you discover you in a way that's both meaningful and fun. She lives in California with her husband, son, and dog, drawing inspiration from the beautiful chaos of family life. To go deeper, you can book a team workshop or find more resources at www.abbeyhowe.com.